New Ways in Teaching Reading

Richard R. Day, Editor

New Ways in TESOL Series:

Innovative Classroom Techniques

Jack C. Richards, Series Editor

Teachers of English to Speakers of Other Languages, Inc.

Typeset in Garamond Book and Tiffany Demi
by Automated Graphic Systems, White Plains, Maryland USA
and printed by
Pantagraph Printing, Bloomington, Illinois USA

Teachers of English to Speakers of Other Languages, Inc.
1600 Cameron Street, Suite 300
Alexandria, Virginia 22314 USA
Tel 703-836-0774 ● Fax 703-836-7864

Director of Communications and Marketing: Helen Kornblum
Senior Editor: Marilyn Kupetz
Cover Design and Spot Art: Ann Kammerer
Part Title Illustrations: David Connell

ISBN 0-939791-45-5
Library of Congress Catalogue No. 93-060127

This book is dedicated to the memory of my parents, Hazel and Henry Day, who taught me the pleasure of reading and got me hooked on books for life.

Contents

Acknowledgments

In a project of this sort, many people deserve thanks. The primary persons to be singled out and recognized are the contributors, those ESL/EFL reading teachers around the world who took time out from their busy lives to share their expertise with others. They did this for no financial gain, being motivated primarily by a desire to share with others the activities and tasks they use in their classrooms.

I would also like to acknowledge the support given me in this project by Naomi Hirata and Marilyn Mitobe, secretaries in the Department of English as a Second Language, University of Hawaii. Appreciation is due Jack C. Richards, Editor of the New Ways in TESOL series, and Helen Kornblum, Director of Communications and Marketing, TESOL Central Office, for their encouragement and advice. Sincere thanks go to Marilyn Kupetz, Senior Editor at TESOL, for her editorial expertise.

Preface

The teaching of reading in second and foreign language contexts is gaining more and more attention, as evidenced by the numerous professional resource books on the topic. This increasing attention is welcome, for reading can be one of the major focuses of learning a second or foreign language.

Becoming an effective and fluent reader in another language has a number of important benefits for the learner. First, reading in the target language helps to consolidate the learning that has taken place. In addition, it may help to increase knowledge of the target language through exposure to new vocabulary and grammatical structures. Reading in the new language is also an important way to learn about the target culture.

Becoming an effective and fluent reader in another language is to acquire a life-long skill, one that helps the student maintain a competence and fluency in the target language that may well outlast competence and fluency in speaking, listening, and writing. Finally, it is a skill that requires only a book or magazine or story, nothing else. And it can be done any place, any time.

It is my belief that the activities and exercises in this volume will help ESL/EFL reading teachers everywhere help their students learn this important and life-long habit.

Richard R. Day
Honolulu, Hawaii

Introduction

This book is a collection of activities, exercises, and suggestions contributed by teachers who have used them in their teaching of reading in ESL and EFL classrooms. It is a resource book for ESL and EFL reading teachers by ESL and EFL reading teachers.

The primary criterion for inclusion in the book was the generalizabilty of the contribution from its use in the contributor's own classroom to the classrooms of other reading teachers. That is, my goal is to offer exercises and activities that are effective in the contributor's classroom and are likely to be just as successful in others as well.

The book is organized into three major divisions: Extensive Reading, Intensive Reading, and Oral Reading. Although there is not complete agreement as to the meaning of the term *extensive reading,* it is used in this book to refer to the teaching of reading through reading. In this approach, there is no overt focus on teaching reading. Rather, it is assumed that the best way for students to learn to read is by reading a great deal of comprehensible material.

In contrast, in the second major division, Intensive Reading, the contributions focus explicitly on some aspect of the teaching of reading. Each of the 16 sections in this division offers specific activities and exercises that relate to a reading skill or situation, from prereading activities to ways in which literature can be used in the reading class. There are many more contributions in the Intensive Reading division than in the other two, which reflects the emphasis the teaching of reading skills has in our profession.

Oral Reading is the theme of the third major division. All of the activities in this division were contributed by Marc Helgesen. It may be unusual to feature oral reading activities, given that most authorities on the teaching of second language reading warn against the practice of having students read aloud in the reading classroom. However, as Helgesen notes in the introduction to the division, oral reading may be an integral part of the teaching of reading, especially in EFL contexts. The activities he proposes make reading aloud more effective by allowing the readers to take part in tasks and activities that help them interact with the reading passage and with each other.

Although the specific focus of the book is the teaching of ESL/EFL reading, many of the activities can be used regardless of the target language. Generally, the only change that would have to be made is to use a reading passage in the target language.

Users' Guide to Activities

Academic Reading

Reading Rate

Literature

Assessment/Evaluation

Vocabulary

Dictionaries

Cohesion

Games for Young Readers

Miscellaneous

Part III: Oral Reading

Part I: Extensive Reading

Tell Us About It

Levels
Beginning +

Aims
Encourage students to
read extensively
Hold students
accountable for out-of-
class reading

Class Time
10 minutes

Preparation Time
None

Resources
Books, magazines,
newspapers

Although out-of-class reading is a school assignment, it can resemble real-world reading if students choose what they want to read and respond to it in their own way, without being tested on it. They are likely to be interested in and inspired by the opinions and reading experiences of their peers but should be held individually accountable for what they read.

Procedure

1. Have students choose their own books (or other material), read them out of class, and then bring them to class.
2. Create groups of 3 students.
3. Ask students in the group to summarize and critique their texts for the other group members. This should be a brief summary of the contents (without giving too much away), an opinion as to the quality of the reading matter, and a recommendation (or not) that others read it. While speaking, students can use the text's cover, headlines, or illustrations as realia to focus their listeners' attention.

Offer beginners the following patterns:

- Introduction: *Last week, I read (title). It is a (type of book), and I (liked/didn't like) it.*
- Body: Brief summary of book or one of the short stories in it, preferably with cliff-hanging ending: *If you want to know what happens, you'll have to read this book.*
- Conclusion: *I (recommend/don't recommend) this book to (every-one/people) who like(s) (type) books.*

As students advance, build other functional language into preparation lessons.

4. If time is tight, have one of the listening students in each group act as timekeeper, giving a 2-minute warning.

Caveats and Options

1. Ask students to submit reports in written form instead of or in addition to speaking about their texts.
2. Do this activity on a regular basis, perhaps once a week, with group members changing each time to encourage students to complete the readings. If more advanced students take more than a week to finish longer books, they can report on newspaper or magazine articles in the interim weeks.

References and Further Reading

Bamford, J. (1984). Extensive reading by means of graded readers. *Reading in a Foreign Language, 2,* 218–260.

Contributor

Julian Bamford, Associate Professor of English Language at Bunkyo University, Chigasaki, Japan, is co-authoring a teacher's handbook on extensive reading.

Book Wheels

Levels
High beginning +

Aims
Encourage students to
think about what they
read
Provide a way for
students to get
suggestions for books
they might want to read

Class Time
25–45 minutes

Preparation Time
45 minutes

Resources
Heavy paper
Spinnable arrows

In this activity, students react affectively to what they read, analyzing and reconstructing the text. They also get to give their classmates advice on books to look for—or avoid. The gamelike nature of the activity encourages even the most reticent students to speak up and share their opinions.

Procedure

1. Cut out wheels from construction paper approximately 1 foot in diameter. Punch a hole in the center of each big enough to insert a spinnable arrow. (If spinnable arrows are not available, use ballpoint pens.)
2. Divide each wheel into 12 even sections. In 10 or 11 sections, write questions appropriate to the type of reading your students will be doing during the semester or year (e.g., fiction, nonfiction, poetry). In the remaining section(s), write, *Please ask your own question.*
3. Make a list of questions similar to the ones that appear on the book wheels.
4. Give the list to your students and ask them to read a book in preparation for playing "Book Wheels."
5. After the students have read at least one book, place them in groups of four.
6. Assign the following roles to each group member:

   The Reporter: tells about the book by answering eight questions from the wheel.
   The Spinner: spins the wheel.
   The Questioner: reads the questions indicated by the spin or, if the arrow lands on *Please ask your own question,* makes up a question.
   The Encourager: prompts reporters to elaborate on their answers.

7. After eight questions have been answered, ask another group member to serve as the Reporter. Rotate the other three roles after each spin of the arrow.

Caveats and Options

1. Assign role of encourager to everyone.
2. Ask the group or the reporter to write a brief response to the book. Circulate these responses to provide the entire class and future classes with advice on what books to read.
3. Generate questions for the book wheels with student participation.
4. Students will probably need practice in answering the questions, in asking their own, and in encouraging others to elaborate. Try to include questions on the wheels that encourage higher order thinking, such as *If you could, how would you change the book's ending?;* that involve feelings, such as *Who was your favorite character? Why?;* and that relate to the lives of your students, such as *How can you use what you learned from the book in your own life?* The idea is for the group discussions to come to resemble conversations that people have about books they read on their own, thereby encouraging them to think about what they read.

References and Further Reading

Laughlin, G. (1987). Book report roulette. In D. W. Johnson, R. T. Johnson, & E. J. Holubec (Eds.), *Structuring cooperative learning: Lesson plans for teachers* (pp. 145–156). Edina, MI: Interaction Book Company.

Contributor

George Jacobs received a doctorate in Educational Psychology from the University of Hawaii. His interests include second language reading and global issues.

Enter Your Selection, Please

Levels
Any

Aims
Encourage students to
read extensively

Class Time
No set time

Preparation Time
Hours, days, weeks,
months!

Resources
Computer, commercial
database, printer
Readability index
formula or software
Reading material

If students only choose books that are appealing to them (e.g., have an attractive cover or an interesting topic), they may choose books that are beyond their reading level, become discouraged with reading, and stop. If extensive reading is a goal of a language program, you may need to direct them to books of appropriate linguistic levels. Databases can help you do this effectively.

Procedure

1. Using the information on the cover or jacket of the book and either a readability formula or readability software, categorize the books you will suggest to your students according to the basic categories of subject matter, genres, readability level, and length. Add any other pertinent categories.
2. Create a reading database of books, preferably the specific books in your library, using any database software.
3. Teach your students how to use the database and/or the computer.
4. The students can spend class or free time using the database. You must consider if the program really encourages or requires the students to spend a lot of time reading extensively, if they are going to use the database frequently enough to justify the time invested, or if they will bypass the database and hunt for books randomly.

Caveats and Options

1. Follow the same procedure using index cards—although a manual database is more difficult to create and not as easy to use.
2. The BookWhiz series (the Educational Testing Service's reading databases for the Apple II) gave me the idea of using a computer database tailored to a particular school library. Christine Nuttall (1987) makes

several suggestions for creating a class library, including the idea of classifying books and coding them for linguistic levels.

References and Further Reading

Nuttall, C. (1987). *Teaching reading skills in a foreign language*. London: Heinemann.

Contributor

David E. Kluge, MA TEFL, San Francisco State University, California and visiting Associate Professor at Kinjo Gakuin University, Nagoya, Japan, is interested in code-switching and CALL.

Your Turn at the Mike

Levels
Any

Aims
Encourage students to
read extensively

Class Time
30 minutes

Preparation Time
30 minutes–1 hour

Resources
Copy or printing
machine
Interview questionnaire

Sharing readings with a partner gives students the pleasure of being an expert in a certain area and encourages them to keep reading. This activity allows them to practice interviewing, reporting, and writing skills.

Procedure

1. Ask students to choose any reading in a particular genre (e.g., poem, newspaper or magazine article, short story, play, long nonfiction) as preparation for an interview on it. You may want to suggest texts of a particular length. Give this reading assignment well in advance of the interview. The number of days or weeks in advance depends on the length of the reading and the students' time constraints. Tell the students to bring the reading to class on the day of the interview.
2. Before the interview day, print enough copies of the interview questionnaire (see Appendix below) so that each student can have one.
3. On the day of the interview, hand out the questionnaires and go over the questions to make sure that students know the vocabulary.
4. Assign each student a partner. One person is the interviewer and asks the other the questions on the questionnaire about the reading. The interviewer writes the answers on the questionnaire sheet. Then the two exchange roles.
5. Ask each student to choose another partner and report what the first partner said about the reading. (I seat my students in a circle, so this step is easy; they just turn to the other person sitting next to them.)

Caveats and Options

1. Ask students to report to the class what their partner said about the reading, with the rest of the students jotting down interesting titles.
2. Ask the interviewer to write a report of the interview to hand in. If the report is first given to the interviewee to check for accuracy, the

activity could then encompass the four skills of speaking, listening, writing, and reading.

3. Post all the questionnaires or reports, or just the favorable ones, so that students can browse and perhaps find their next book.

Appendix: Sample Interview Questionnaire

Directions: Put each set of question prompts on a separate sheet with adequate space after each prompt for the answer. For lower level students, use actual questions instead of question prompts.

1. Magazine Reading Interview

Ask your partner

- what the name of the magazine is
- what the title of the article is
- who the author of the article is
- what the article is about
- if s/he liked the article
- why s/he liked the article, or why s/he didn't like the article
- what message s/he got from the article

2. Long Nonfiction Reading Interview

Ask your partner

- what the title of the nonfiction is
- who the author of the nonfiction is
- what kind of nonfiction it is (diary/journal, biography, autobiography, essay, etc.)
- what the nonfiction is about
- if s/he liked the nonfiction
- why s/he liked the nonfiction, or why not
- what message s/he got from the nonfiction

3. Novel/Play Reading Interview

Ask your partner

- if s/he read a novel or a play
- what the title of the novel or play is

- what kind of novel or play it is (e.g., adventure, romance, historical, fantasy/science fiction, mystery, horror)
- what the novel or play is about
- if s/he liked the novel or play
- why s/he liked it, or why not
- what main message s/he got from this novel or play
- if s/he would recommend this novel or play to you

4. Poem Reading Interview

Ask your partner

- what the title of the poem is
- who the author of the poem is
- to read the poem to you
- what the poem is about
- if s/he liked the poem
- why s/he liked the poem or why not
- what main message s/he got from the poem

5. Short Story Reading Interview

Ask your partner

- what the title of the short story is
- who the author of the short story is
- what kind of short story it is
- what the short story is about
- if s/he liked the short story
- why s/he liked it, or why not
- what main message s/he got from this story
- if s/he would recommend this story to you

Contributor

David E. Kluge, MA TEFL, San Francisco State University, California and visiting Associate Professor at Kinjo Gakuin University, Nagoya, Japan, is interested in code-switching and CALL.

Universal Questions

Levels
Intermediate +

Aims
Provide a framework for generic testing of reading comprehension

Class Time
No specific time

Preparation Time
Longer than if each member of the class reads the same text

Students are usually faced with a prepackaged group of texts for their ESL courses. Although this may be necessary for controlling the level of difficulty, for example, it can add to student apathy. Older students should be allowed some independence in choosing texts; university students should have an opportunity to read texts that relate to their own fields. This allows them to express their opinions by discussing a text without the limitations imposed by traditional reading comprehension questions.

Procedure

1. Teach students to discern rhetorical structure in texts. (See the activities in Organization and Structure, this volume; see also the references at the end of this activity.) Screen articles in advance for appropriateness of level and content.
2. Distribute the questionnaire for analytic and descriptive articles (see Appendix below).

References and Further Reading

Carrell, P. L. (1985). Facilitating ESL reading by teaching text structure. *TESOL Quarterly, 19*, 727–752.

Lewin, B. (in press). A schema-based reading test. *Issues in Language Teaching*. Tel Aviv University.

Appendix: Sample Questionnaire

Directions: If any questions are not applicable to your article (i.e., the information doesn't appear), write NA in the appropriate space. Answer the questions in your own words.

1. What is the topic of your article?

2. What was the author's purpose in writing this article?
3. a. If the article is an argument:
      What is the author's thesis?
      Is it explicitly stated in the text? If so, where?
   b. If the article is an analysis: What is/are the main idea(s) about the topic?
4. Give at least two examples or pieces of evidence from the text which support the author's thesis/main idea.
5. Do you think that the author has adequately supported his/her thesis? Why or why not?
   If not, what kind of support did the author leave out?
6. Is the author mainly objective or mainly subjective? What clues led you to your conclusion (e.g., word choice, analogies)?
7. Write an outline of the article (maximum one page). Follow the structure we studied in class.
8. What new fact or idea did you learn from this article?
9. Does the author refute anyone else's theories (or "the common idea")? If so, what is the rejected idea?

Caveats and Options

The questionnaire is adaptable to different rhetorical structures. Two sets of questions for other forms follow.

For a problem/solution article:

1. Describe the problem. Include the extent, scope, seriousness of the problem.
2. What are the causes of the problem?

For a research article:

1. What social or theoretical problem led the authors to do this study?
2. What is the main difference between the authors' research and previous research?

Contributors

Beverly A. Lewin and Joyce Friedler are coordinators of the English for Humanities program in the Division of Foreign Languages, Tel Aviv University, Israel.

Lending Library

Levels
Beginning; secondary

Aims
Promote sustained
silent reading using
student-selected reading
materials

Class Time
20–30 minutes

Preparation Time
None, after classroom
library is assembled

Resources
Traditional children's
and elementary school-
level books

The way you present reading material influences how students receive it. The joy the students experience in being able to read beyond their own expectations usually overrides any apprehension they have about the appropriateness of the material. The illustrations and stories in many children's books delight both young and old, as most parents who are reading to their children can attest.

Procedure

1. After collecting enough books for your purposes, spread them out and ask students to select the ones that they want to read.
2. Let students read to themselves for 20–30 minutes. If the book they have selected is too difficult or not of interest to them, let them choose another. Explain that they do not need to understand every word but should try to figure out the story. Encourage students to consult you if they find recurring unfamiliar words that seem important to their overall understanding.
3. When the reading period is over, ask students to return the books to the table. Don't give comprehension or vocabulary tests and don't ask the students to read aloud in front of the class. Let them read for their own enjoyment.

Caveats and Options

1. It is important to have materials available in a wide range of content and difficulty so that the students can pick something that is right for them.
2. If school funds to purchase books are not available, other sources include school and public libraries, book sales at public libraries,

garage sales, specially targeted federal and state funds, small grants for teachers, used book stores and thrift shops, and book clubs.

Contributor

Holbrook Mahn, a doctoral student in the TESOL program at the University of New Mexico, taught ESL at Belmont High School in Los Angeles, California for 3 years.

Taking a Cloze Look

Levels
Intermediate +

Aims
Evaluate a course in
extensive reading

Test Time
1 hour

Preparation Time
2 hours

Resources
Short stories and essays
from graded readers
and young adult
literature

A cloze test measures learners' global proficiency in vocabulary, grammar, and reading comprehension. The task is holistic and therefore ideal for evaluating the results of an extensive reading program.

Procedure

I. Preparing the Test

1. Before the course begins, select a story or essay at the reading level you want your students to achieve by the end of the course. Have a few teachers who speak the students' native language read the story or essay and evaluate the difficulty.
2. Make sure the content of the testing text is completely unfamiliar to the students; otherwise it will become a test of grammar.
3. Set the length of the passage at 1,500–2,000 words.
4. Delete every 10th word.
5. Do not delete anything from the first paragraph. This gives students some background knowledge of the text and helps them to use the first paragraph to create an understanding of the text.
6. Prepare 100 items. This may seem an unusually large number of items, but reliability is improved in this way. The reading level of difficulty should be high when the test is given at the beginning of the course. The average score of the pretest should be below 35 points.
7. Give the test to your students at the beginning of the course, as a pretest. You might want to number the copies to make sure that none turn up missing.
8. Give the test again after 2 weeks as a reliability check. If you are teaching more than two classes, choose any one of them to retest for this purpose.

9. Determine the reliability of the test; if satisfactory, at least $r = .85$, give the test again as a posttest at the end of the course.
10. Run a T test to find out if the gain is significant.

II. Grading the Test

1. Have several native speakers take the test to see what variety of words can be used for each blank, in addition to those used in the original text.
2. Have a few native-speaker teachers look at the students' test papers to see if they can find any more suitable words for the blanks.
3. Make a master list of acceptable answers for each deletion.
4. Do not tell the students in advance that they will take the same test as a posttest because you don't want them to get together to prepare.

Caveats and Options

1. In order to make a reliable test, it is better to pretest the instrument at your school to see if you can use it the following year for your students. The quality of your students won't change that much from one year to the next.
2. Once you establish a fairly good test, you can use it every year. The test can then become a standardized test for your school.

Contributors

Beniko Mason and Tom Pendergast have been teaching and administering an extensive reading program at Shitennoji International Buddhist University, in Osaka, Japan, for the past 8 years.

Getting the Point

Levels
Intermediate +

Aims
Have students learn to
summarize stories orally
Practice recognizing
main ideas and
identifying plot and
characters in a story

Class Time
20 minutes

Preparation Time
No set time

We often want to share our reaction to stories we have read with others. This activity encourages students to talk about what they've read and lets them practice the language and communication skills they need to do that.

Procedure

1. Tell the class that they will have 10 minutes during the following class period to tell a classmate about a book that they have read.
2. Tell them to include the following information in their reports:

   - Title and author
   - Main characters
   - Plot
   - Outcome
   - Their opinion or recommendation

3. To make sure that they understand the assignment, model an oral report about a book you have read for the class.
4. The following day, divide the class into pairs. Give each person 10 minutes to report and answer any questions from the other person. Tell them that they can refer to notes but that they cannot read from their notes. Encourage them to look at their partners when they are speaking. Encourage the listeners to ask questions to make sure that they understand. Help them understand they are communicating something interesting, so they should act that way.
5. After 10 minutes, have the partners switch roles.

Caveats and Options

1. Have the students write a report of their oral summary, either as homework or as an in-class assignment, but limit the amount that

the students can write. For example, begin with a paragraph and then gradually increase the length requirement to a page or so during the semester or year.

2. Urge them to use their own words and not to copy sentences from the books. Also, encourage them to write in English, rather than translating from their first language.

3. It is helpful to save the first summaries and compare them to the final summaries the students do at the end of the course. This way you can tell if the students have improved.

Contributors

Beniko Mason and Tom Pendergast have been teaching and administering an extensive reading program at Shitennoji International Buddhist University, in Osaka, Japan, for the past 8 years.

Reading and Vocabulary Log

Levels
Intermediate +

Aims
Practice independent
reading strategies
Explore reading
resources

Class Time
20–30 minutes

Preparation Time
30 minutes–1 hour

Resources
Reading material chosen
by you and your
students

If ESL students increase their exposure to a variety of reading materials, they may find enough to interest them that reading in English will become part of their daily lives—outside of class. This activity asks them to focus on why they chose a particular text and what they thought about it.

Procedure

1. Introduce a model of a completed reading log (see Appendix below) and some sample reading materials.
2. Ask students to select their own reading material and fill in the log each week.
3. Have students discuss logs in class in small groups or use them as a basis for a presentation to the class. They can bring their source material to class to share.

Appendix: Weekly Reading and Vocabulary Log

Date: Name:
Log number: Class:
Title of book, magazine, or newspaper:
Chapter of book, or title of short story or article:
Year book or story was published, or date of magazine or newspaper:
Author of book, story, or article (newspaper articles may not have one):
Number of pages you read (or columns of a newspaper):
How long did it take you to read this?
Where did you get this reading material from? (school or public library, your home, a friend, a bookstore or magazine shop)
Why did you choose this reading material?

Briefly, tell me what you read about: (Write a summary, outline or mind map.)

What did this reading selection make you think about or how did it make you feel?

Are you glad you chose to read this or are you sorry about your choice? Why do you feel this way?

Was this reading selection too easy, too hard, or just right for you? What makes you think so?

List three new vocabulary words you learned. Based on the context in the reading, include the part of speech (N, V, Adj, Adv), meaning, and a sentence of your own for each word.

    1.

    2.

    3.

Contributor

Claudine Poggi has been teaching ESL since 1976. Affiliated with DeAnza College in Cupertino, California, she has presented at TESOL and California TESOL (CATESOL) conferences and contributes to CATESOL publications.

Eight Steps to an ESOL Collection

Levels
Any

Aims
Offer nonnative speakers access to simplified books in a public library

Preparation Time
Extensive

Resources
Simplified reading material of all kinds

A special ESOL section in a public library can offer books whose subject matter is not childish or patronizing to adults, yet which has been adapted or simplified according to accepted word-frequency levels. In an ESOL reading section, most books are short stories or novels. Because it is unlikely that potential readers (ESOL students) would find them if they were shelved with the rest of the library's fiction collection, it is better to shelve them in a separate section, highlighted as *ESOL.*

Basic-, intermediate-, and advanced-level books are shelved separately as well. Books labeled *Basic* are between 300–1,000 words, *Low-intermediate* between 1,000–2,000 words, *High-intermediate* between 2,000–3,000 words, and *Advanced* between 3,000–7,000 words. These levels generally fit the ESOL publishers' classification.

Instead of being organized by author, the books are alphabetized by title. This is the way the books are listed in catalogues, but it is not normal library procedure. However, it does not really matter if the books stay in order, as long as they are grouped according to different word levels. Students can browse among them all, experimenting as they go along.

Another special feature of an ESOL collection is the way the books are checked out of the library. If they are catalogued as ordinary books, the author and the title will be recorded electronically along with the user's library card when a book is taken out. However, it is a good idea upon starting a collection to learn how many times a book circulates during the year, and the usual check-out system does not record this. You may wish to return to the old-fashioned system of having a slip pasted on the book's end flap, with blanks for a date-due stamp. The circulation-desk employees can be alerted to the special system by a prominent ESOL sticker on the right-hand cover of the book.

Procedure

1. Determine need. What is the foreign student, visitor, immigrant population in your area?
2. Approach the library with a tentative proposal. Make an appointment with the library director. Take lists, catalogues, sample readers.
3. Decide on a budget. In the United States, for example, 100 paperback ESOL readers currently cost about $500. Start with 50 titles.
4. Order books. Look at ESOL publishers' catalogues, noting everything labeled reader. Check descriptions; note word levels. Look for balance between basic, intermediate, and advanced. Use these criteria for selection: adult? adapted? short stories? short novels? inexpensive paperbacks? Content: entertaining? suspenseful? detective story? historical? biographical?
5. Divide duties. Decide which tasks the library will do, which you will do. Tasks include ordering, marking books, pasting date-due sheets, typing file cards, and publicizing the collection.
6. Catalogue, shelve, get ready to circulate. When orders arrive, check over books and mark each level. (Suggested word levels: basic 300–1,000; low-intermediate 1,000–2,000; high-intermediate 2,000–3,000; advanced 3,000–7,000.)

   Two catalogue file cards are needed for each book, both showing title, author, publisher, year, and word-level. List books in the first card file by levels, alphabetically by title. In the second card file, list all books alphabetically by title. (First card file for students to use; second card file for administration to keep.)

   Shelve separately from other fiction. Three small shelves approximately 1 yard wide each are adequate for 200 ESOL paperbacks.

7. Publicize. Take pictures of ESOL students looking at books. Write a short, newsy article. Have the library send the release to local papers. Give out one-page flyers to your students and schools. Let other organizations distribute flyers.
8. Keep up collection. Take inventory once a year. Replace worn-out or lost books. Add new books. Gradually expand the collection and add second copies.

References and Further Reading

Shanefield, L. (1986, October). ESOL at the library: How to set up a collection. *TESOL Newsletter,* pp. 1, 5.

Contributor

Libby Shanefield, a charter member of TESOL, is President of Princeton ESOL Consultants. She teaches adults at all levels, with a focus on the English needs of professionals.

Reading Questionnaire

Levels
Any

Aims
Make students aware of
their reading habits so
that they can address
ineffective ones

Class Time
30–45 minutes

Preparation Time
30 minutes

Resources
Reading questionnaire

Before students can become efficient readers, they must become aware of their reading habits—good and bad. A reading questionnaire helps them focus on what they do, why, and what you and they might be able to address together.

Procedure

1. Distribute a questionnaire similar to the one in the Appendix below.
2. Collect completed questionnaires from students.
3. In the next class, report the results and discuss good and bad reading habits.

Caveats and Options

This activity should be done during the first class session so that the results can be used for diagnosis.

Appendix:
Reading
Questionnaire

Reading

1. What do you think a good reader does? A good reader
   (a) reads fast
   (b) understands all the words
   (c) makes guesses
   (d) always reads carefully
   (e) does other things _____

Reading in Your First Language
   1. Do you like reading?
   2. How often do you read?
   3. When and where do you read?

4. What kinds of things do you read? (e.g., newspapers, magazines, novels, comics...)
5. What do you like to read about?

Reading in English
1. Do you like reading in English?
2. How often do you read in English?
3. What kinds of things do you like to read or would you like to read in English?
4. What do you or would you like to read about in English?

English Reading Habits
1. Do you read slowly?
   (a) rarely
   (b) sometimes
   (c) often
   (d) always
2. Do you translate into Japanese?
   (a) rarely
   (b) sometimes
   (c) often
   (d) always
3. Do you look up unfamiliar words?
   (a) rarely
   (b) sometimes
   (c) often
   (d) always
4. Do you read aloud?
   (a) rarely
   (b) sometimes
   (c) often
   (d) always

Contributor

Eiko Ujitani has an MA in EFL from Southern Illinois University and teaches at Nagoya University of Foreign Studies in Japan.

Judging a Book by Its Cover

Levels
Any

Aims
Teach students skimming so they can find interesting books

Class Time
30–45 minutes

Preparation Time
10 minutes

Resources
Books unfamiliar to the students, preferably with attractive pictures and summaries on their covers

The table of contents and the pictures on the front and back covers usually carry a lot of information about a book. If students pay attention to these features, they can choose what they want to read more efficiently.

Procedure

1. Divide the class into pairs.
2. Circulate a box with books and have each pair choose books they want to look at.
3. Read questions appropriate for skimming. Possible questions include:
   - What's the title?
   - Who is the author?
   - What type of book is it?
   - When and where does the story take place? (for fiction)
   - What is it about? (for nonfiction)
   - Do you feel like reading it? Why or why not?
4. Ask pairs to write answers for each book.
5. Ask several pairs to report answers back to class.

Contributor

Eiko Ujitani has an MA in EFL from Southern Illinois University and teaches at Nagoya University of Foreign Studies in Japan.

Writing a Book Report

Levels
Any

Aims
Encourage students to read and express their views

Class Time
No set time

Preparation Time
Minimal

Resources
Book report form

In an extensive reading course, a teacher needs to check that students have read enough texts and have learned something from their reading. By reporting their reactions to a book, students can demonstrate comprehension and encourage their peers to find and read interesting books.

Procedure

1. Have students fill out a book report form (see Appendix below) every time they finish a book.
2. Have students cut the report along the line, filing the top half in their own folder and handing in the bottom half to the teacher.

Caveats and Options

1. Choose several interesting reports and display them for the class.
2. Ask students to tell the class or each other about their reactions to a book based on their book reports.

Appendix: Book Report Form

Name:
Title: Publisher:
Date borrowed:
Date returned:

....

Title:
Did you like the book? It was
____ Great
____ Good
____ OK
____ Boring

Would you recommend this book to your classmates?
Why or why not?

Contributor

Eiko Ujitani has an MA in EFL from Southern Illinois University and teaches at Nagoya University of Foreign Studies in Japan.

Part II: Intensive Reading

◆ Prereading
Asking the Right Questions

Levels
Intermediate +

Aims
Help students survey an article before reading and create a structure for the type of information they will find
Prepare students to read authentic texts from magazines and newspapers

Class Time
30 minutes–1 hour

Preparation Time
30 minutes

Resources
Any mainstream newspaper or magazine

Students comprehend text more easily if they have a clear idea about what kind of information they can expect to encounter. Surveying the titles (or headings), subtitles (or subheadings), graphics, and first and last paragraphs helps students sort out what will not be included and focus on what will. Because news articles include so much information in their opening paragraphs and headings, they are a good resource for this sort of activity.

Procedure

1. Locate one current, short to medium-length article that includes subtitles and some kind of graphics (e.g., charts, graphs).
2. From one copy of the article, cut out the titles, subtitles, graphics, the first paragraph, and the last paragraph.
3. Lay out these items on a sheet of paper in a logical way, for example, title followed by first paragraph, subtitles in order with some space in between, last paragraph at the end, graphics to the side. In other words, try to mirror the "look" of the article (minus the main body of words).
4. Form the class into small groups or pairs and ask them to survey these items briefly.
5. Ask student groups or pairs to write 5–10 questions that they believe will be answered by the body of the article.
6. Ask groups or pairs to share sample questions with whole class. Discuss why the article probably will or will not answer each question. The focus here is to get the students to note what information in the survey indicates the direction the article will take.
7. Have students read a copy of the entire article and then answer their own questions.

8. Discuss with the whole class which questions did not get answered and why.

Caveats and Options

1. While half the class writes the questions, ask the other half to read the article. Then have the first half ask the questions and the second half tries to answer the questions. Discuss which questions did not get answered and why. Repeat on another day with another article, but switch student roles.
2. The main features of this activity are the survey, the writing of questions, and the discussion about which questions worked. It is up to the individual teacher how extensively to deal with the actual reading of the article.

Contributor

Allen Ascher, Assistant Director of the International English Language Institute at Hunter College, City University of New York, has taught ESL in the United States and EFL in China.

Ten Things to Do Before Reading

Levels
Any

Aims
Practice previewing

Class Time
10 minutes

Preparation Time
Little or none

Resources
Reading passages from students' books

Before students begin any reading passage, they need to preview it to see what they already know in terms of content and vocabulary. Previewing makes for smoother reading and smoother reading lessons. Any one of the following directions, or a combination, may be used each time a new passage is introduced.

Procedure

1. Ask students to brainstorm for answers to the following questions, then write ideas on the board.
   - Look at the title and the headings for each section. What do you think this passage is going to be about?
   - Look at the pictures. What do you think this passage is going to be about?
   - Read the first and last paragraphs and the first sentence of each paragraph. What do you think this passage is going to be about?
   - Read the title. Now quickly scan the passage and circle all the words that have a connection to the title.
   - Scan the passage and cross out all the words you don't know. After you read the passage again carefully, look up the words in a dictionary.
   - After looking at the title, pictures, and so on, brainstorm the specific words you expect to see in the passage.
   - After looking at the title and pictures, make up some questions you think this passage might answer.
   - What kind of passage is this? (fiction? nonfiction—what kind?) Why would somebody read this? For information? Pleasure?

2. Choose words from the passage and write them on the board. Ask students to scan the passage and circle them (to give preteaching of vocabulary a task).
3. Tell a story about the background of the reading passage, or summarize the passage itself. Ask students to take notes or draw a picture of the story as you speak.
4. Have everyone read the passage.

Contributor

Steven Brown is on the staff of the University of Pittsburgh English Language Institute in Pennsylvania. He is a co-author of the English Firsthand *and* English Firsthand Beginners' Course *text series.*

Teaching Transitions

Levels
High beginning +

Aims
Introduce students to
transitions and how to
use them to read
effectively

Class Time
15–20 minutes

Preparation Time
10–30 minutes

Resources
Reading passages in
students' textbook or
other similar sources

Efficient reading entails making accurate predictions and understanding transitions helps students predict organizational patterns and the types of information they will probably find. Because this activity is recursive, students can try it with increasingly sophisticated texts.

Procedure

1. Teach students about types of transitions used in English, using explanations and examples. The following selection is organized by meaning:
   - Additional information: *and, furthermore, moreover, in addition, also*
   - Expected information: *of course, naturally, surely*
   - Unexpected information: *surprisingly, amazingly*
   - Intensified information: *in fact, as a matter of fact*
   - Restatement: *as I mentioned before, in short, in other words, i.e., that is*
   - Example: *for example, for instance, to illustrate, such as*
   - Consequence: *so, therefore, as a result, consequently*
   - Cause/Effect: *because, due to, thanks to, on account of, as a result of, in view of*
   - Contrasting information: *however, but, although, even though, nevertheless*
   - Order: *first, second, then, next*
   - Conclusion: *in short, therefore, in conclusion, in summary, on the whole*
2. Have students make sentences using transitions.
3. Give students a reading passage with the transitions marked. Have the students identify the types of transitions.

4. Have students identify the transitions in a reading passage and the type of transition.
5. Give students a reading passage with the transitions deleted. Have students fill in the blanks with appropriate transitions and identify the type of transition they have used. (In some cases, it will be possible to use more than one type of transition.)
6. Give students a text on a familiar topic with the information following the transitions whited out. Have students predict what would be likely to be in the blanks. (It is necessary to emphasize that they will not always be exactly right; the point is to think about what is likely to be coming.)

Caveats and Options

1. These six steps are basic. However, after the first step, some of the rest can be either skipped or repeated, depending on the proficiency of the class and how well they seem to be doing.
2. Steps 4–6 can be repeated periodically for review purposes even after all six steps have been finished.

Contributor

S. Kathleen Kitao teaches at Doshisha Women's College in Tanabe, Kyoto, Japan.

Weaving the Web

Levels
Beginning +

Aims
Activate students'
knowledge of linguistic
and rhetorical
structures

Class Time
45 minutes–1 hour

Preparation Time
None

Resources
Any reading passage

Webbing, or clustering, is often used as an aid in preparing to write a paper, but it can also help students bring to bear their knowledge of the topic of a reading to improve reading comprehension. Webbing generates key vocabulary, taps into students' prior knowledge of a topic, may bring up a few things some students don't know, generates predictions about what may be covered in the reading, and can prepare students for the type of discourse they will encounter.

Procedure

1. Write the topic of the reading passage on the board.
2. Ask the students what they already know about the topic and what they want to know about it. Write their answers on the board around the topic to create a web (see Appendix below). Try to group similar ideas together.
3. After the students have generated as many ideas as they can, ask them to organize the web into major topics and subtopics, making sure to group similar ideas together.
4. Have them then put topics and subtopics into some kind of logical order (e.g., chronological, cause and effect, comparison and contrast, statement and reason).
5. Have them read the passage.

Appendix: Culture Shock Web

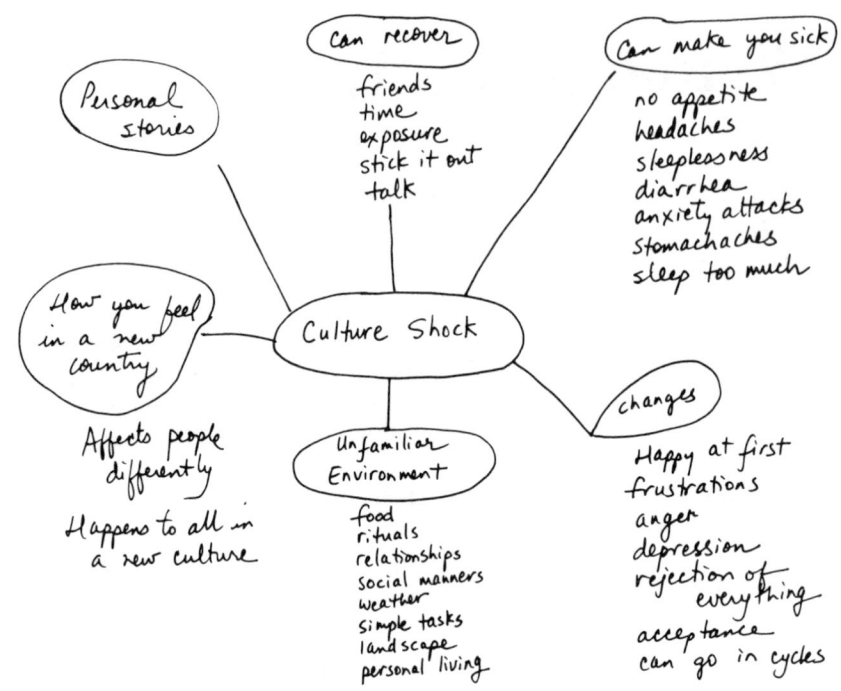

Contributor

Melinda Roth Sayavedra, ESL teacher-educator at Oregon State University in Corvallis, has taught preliterate to advanced university students in the United States and elsewhere for 14 years.

If You Don't Know, Ask, OK?

Levels
Intermediate +

Aims
Encourage students to
think about the topic of
a passage before
reading it
Motivate students to
read
Provide a purpose for
reading

Class Time
15–30 minutes

Preparation Time
Enough to choose a
reading selection

Resources
Short article or news
item from newspaper or
magazine

The more students look forward to reading and anticipate what a text holds in store for them, the easier it will be for them to comprehend its main points. In this prereading activity, students are made aware of what they know, what they don't know, and what they want to know about the topic of a reading selection.

Procedure

1. Announce the topic of the article or news item and ask students to volunteer what they know about it. Encourage students to ask questions.
2. Place the students in groups of three to four and ask them to write at least three questions about the topic.
3. Tell the students that they are going to read an article (or news item) in which some of their questions may be answered. The questions may be answered directly, by inference, or not at all. Their task is to determine what answers, if any, are given to their question.
4. Distribute the reading selection. Students read the selection and look for answers to their group's questions.
5. Have volunteers read their group's questions to the class and report on answers provided in the reading selection.
6. If students have generated questions for which there are no answers in the reading passage, use these as topics for project work or library research.

Caveats and Options

1. Instead of announcing the topic of the selection, read the first two or three sentences of the selection to the class. Be sure that the students understand what the topic is. Elicit questions and write them on the board before distributing the reading selection.

2. Write the title of the reading selection on the board. Tell students to use the title as a basis for forming their questions.

Contributor

Susan Stempleski, a teacher, teacher-trainer and materials developer, co-authored Explorations, Getting Together, *the* Hello, America *multimedia series, and the award-winning* Video in Action. *She co-edited* Video in Second Language Teaching: Using, Selecting, and Producing Video for the Classroom.

Heading + Picture = Main Idea

Levels
Beginning +

Aims
Teach students how to
infer main ideas from
chapter headings and
visual cues
Make students aware of
global issues

Class Time
30 minutes

Preparation Time
30 minutes

Resources
*50 Simple Things You
Can Do To Save the
Earth* or other ecology-
related books with
chapter headings and
pictures

It is important for students to pay more attention to visual cues because they can infer main ideas from them. Books on environmental issues usually have a lot of illustrations, so they work very well in this sort of activity.

Survival of the Rarest

Procedure

1. Choose interesting chapter headings.
2. Copy pictures from those chapters and place them in random order.
3. Create a list of the main ideas, one from each chapter, also in random order.
4. Distribute handouts to students and ask them to match the chapter heading with the picture and then with the main idea.

Caveats and Options

Ask students to write a short paragraph about what an individual can do to save the earth.

Contributor

Eiko Ujitani has an MA in EFL from Southern Illinois University and teaches at Nagoya University of Foreign Studies in Japan.

◆ Prediction
Predicting Rhetorical Structure

Levels
Intermediate +

Aims
Practice prediction of
rhetorical structure of a
text

Class Time
10–20 minutes

Preparation Time
10 minutes

Resources
Any appropriate text

When readers have some idea of what the overall rhetorical structure of a text is, they have a ready-made context for interpreting hierarchies of ideas as well as vocabulary. This activity asks students to skim titles and subtitles for clues to how the text is organized.

Procedure

1. Introduce possible rhetorical structures of each new text as appropriate:
   - Narrative
   - Generalization/example
   - Advice/reason
   - Chronology
   - Problem/solution. . .
2. Have students guess the overall rhetorical structure from the title and subtitles of the reading.
3. Have the students individually skim the article and find evidence for or against their choice.
4. In small groups, ask them to compare their guesses.
5. In a large group, ask them to present their conclusions. Have them write the title of the article on the blackboard, erasing words that would change the overall rhetorical structure. As a class, have them guess and substantiate using the words in the title.

Caveats and Options

1. Divide the article into sections and have small groups scan the section and compare their findings with those of other groups.

2. Best used to introduce a reading, this term-long activity doesn't necessarily have to be done for every reading. The first few times it is done, it is a good idea to explain the overall structure.

Contributor

James Edwin Bame is a lecturer at the Intensive English Language Institute, Utah State University in Logan, Utah. His interests are discourse analysis, listening, and reading.

A Psychological Guessing Game

Levels
Intermediate +

Aims
Practice predicting the next word

Class Time
20–30 minutes

Preparation Time
30 minutes

Resources
Any short text at a suitable reading level

Comprehension can be defined as linking new information to what we know. Thus, we understand texts by using our knowledge of the world, the content area, and the context involved, as well as our knowledge of semantics, syntax, morphology, and orthography, for example. In other words, the reader makes predictions, looks for matches with the predictions, and, upon finding matches, understands. When matches between the prediction and reality do not occur, the reader must backtrack and discover why the prediction did not work.

Procedure

1. Find a passage of appropriate difficulty.
2. Put a typed version of the passage on an overhead transparency.
3. Explain to the students that reading may be a guessing game in which good readers predict the word or phrase that will come next, and then check to see if their prediction is correct. These predictions are done very quickly and looking at every word is not necessary.
4. Start the exercise by projecting the transparency covered with a sheet of paper that is notched as follows:

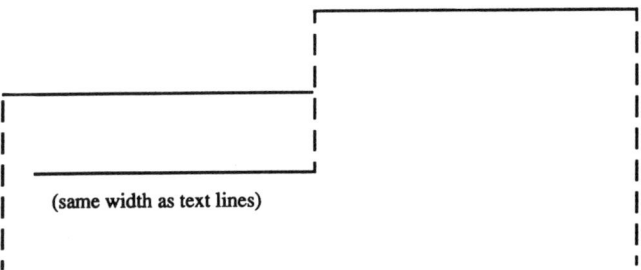

(same width as text lines)

5. Tell the students to number a sheet of paper, listing the predictions you want them to make.
6. Explain to the students that, when you stop moving the paper, you want them to write down their best prediction for the word that will come next.
7. Disclose one portion of the passage at a time (you may want to mark the stopping points in advance so that you can control what will be predicted, or simply stop randomly as you move down the transparency). Allow about 15 seconds for each prediction.
8. When you move the paper to the next stopping place, have the students check their previous answer and then make a new prediction. Repeat this step until all of the predictions (that you want to do) have been made.

Caveats and Option

1. This exercise can also be done on computer software, using Chomsky and Schwartz (1984) or similar software. The advantage of using a computer is that the predictions and feedback will be almost instantaneous.
2. There are numerous other potential exercises that can be developed around the idea of prediction as practiced in cloze; Larson (1979) presents four ways to do so in pair work.

References and Further Reading

Chomsky, C., & Schwartz, J. L. (1984). *M-SS-NG L-NKS*. Pleasantville, NY: Sunburst Communications.

Larson, D. (1979, April). Reading up to expectations. *TESOL Newsletter*, pp. 17, 29.

Contributor

J. D. Brown is on the faculty of the Department of ESL at the University of Hawaii. He has published numerous articles on language testing and curriculum development and a book on critically reading statistical studies, Understanding Research in Second Language Learning.

Reciprocal Questioning

Levels
Intermediate +

Aims
Encourage students to
ask questions in order
to predict what might
happen in a story

Class Time
30 minutes

Preparation Time
30 minutes

Resources
Preferably a story with
a twist ending

It is important that students learn to read with a purpose, predict, and ask themselves high-level questions. When they have acquired these skills, they will be able to read independently and with enjoyment. This activity uses stories with surprise endings to enhance the pleasure of having predicted right.

Procedure

1. Reveal only the title of the selection. This can be done by using an overhead projector, by instructing the students to fold a one-page selection, or by using a cover sheet on a textbook.
2. Ask the students what they think the article is about.
3. Write students' predictions on the board.
4. Tell the class about the activity. Have the students read only one line (or paragraph in the case of longer text) at a time. Then have them ask you any questions they want about that line (or paragraph). Next, ask them questions.
5. Reveal one sentence of the story at a time, proceeding according to the following directions.
6. Allow time for silent, independent reading of the sentence or paragraph.
7. Take turns asking questions. First the students ask you questions, then you ask them.
8. Model good questioning techniques each time it is your turn. Ask any of five types of questions, using prediction questions and the acronym *FIVE*:

    *F*actual questions: Those that are directly answered in the story. (e.g., *What was the girl's name?*)

*I*nference questions: Those where a guess will have to be made. (e.g., *Why do you think the boys were afraid to go in the cemetery?*)

*V*ocabulary questions: Those which reveal knowledge or lack of it about the words in the story. (e.g., *What does the word cemetery mean?*)

*E*xperience questions: Those that help students draw on their own background with the subject (e.g., *Have you ever had a sick friend?*)

9. When students ask questions, give appropriate feedback on their questioning behavior. For example, if a student asks a question for which no answer was given in the story, you might reply, "I don't know. It doesn't say." However, if a student asks an inference question, you could model the process of thinking of possible answers.

10. Continue the reciprocal questioning line-by-line or paragraph-by-paragraph, revising previous predictions and adding others when appropriate, until the main idea or plot of the article or story is revealed. Ask students to read the rest of the selection silently. I have found that if a story with a surprise ending has been used, the students often laugh aloud when they realize that their predictions were wrong. In this way they learn that wrong predictions aren't "bad" predictions.

11. When students have finished their reading, revise the predictions listed on the blackboard.

Caveats and Options

1. This adaptation of Anthony Manzo's (1964) ReQuest Procedure is enjoyable because of its gamelike nature. However, potential problems must be considered. For example, in the story "The Flowers," three boys give their sick friend flowers stolen from a grave. The twist comes when the dead man comes to claim his flowers! For some cultures, Navajo in particular, disturbing the resting place of the dead would be not just dishonest, but sacrilegious. The twist ending would not be considered humorous. Another example with a surprise ending is O. Henry's "The Gift of the Magi." Inference and experience questions about the main characters' unselfish but sentimental motives might be meaningless to a more practical Asian culture. Often what seems a twist ending to the teacher may not

be to the students of another culture. Added to this is the problem of locating many stories at the class's reading level that have self-defined prediction points.

2. A solution to these problems is to move on soon to regular classroom texts. After a few experiences with ReQuest, when the students are familiar with prediction and inferential questions, it is not difficult to move to more readily available, culturally appropriate material. You can devise activities involving groups, pairs or individual students in forming inferential and predictive questions for stories in their regular reading material. For example, students might be asked to formulate predictions or inferential questions after looking at illustrations accompanying the written material, after reading the title, after being presented with the theme or thesis of the selection, or after reading the first paragraph. In addition, students could exchange predictions and questions. Then after reading the selection independently they could be asked to find possible evidence in the story for answers to the inferential questions.

3. When students move into less gamelike activities, it is advisable to reinforce the high-level inferential thinking by direct teaching of the acronym FIVE. This helps to keep students from using only literal questions.

4. Students can be asked to write questions with predicted answers for chunks of nonfiction material. After reading a subtitle or the first sentence in a paragraph in a science text, students could write questions they think will be answered in that section.

5. Cooper and Petrosky (1976) have suggested that predictive and questioning strategies are used by good readers in their native languages. By direct teaching of effective reader-generated questioning techniques, ESL students can learn to use their predictive and questioning abilities in English. ReQuest allows independent student/text interaction, emphasizing high-level questioning and deemphasizing trivial fact parroting.

References and Further Reading

Cooper, C. R., & Petrosky, A. R. (1976). A psycholinguistic view of the fluent reading process. *Journal of Reading, 20,* 184–207.

Manzo, A. V. (1969). The ReQuest procedure. *Journal of Reading, 13,* 126–136.

Contributor

Allene Cooper is Program Coordinator of the Writing Across the Curriculum Program at Arizona State University in Tempe. She has been President of Arizona TESOL and has taught ESL at university and community colleges.

Vocabulary Sort

Levels
Beginning +

Aims
Promote basic
understanding of new
vocabulary through
prediction strategies

Class Time
15 minutes

Preparation Time
15 minutes

Resources
Large sheets of chart
paper
20–30 small pieces of
paper

Students who are actively involved in predicting the meaning of new vocabulary will have a better understanding of the text and be more motivated to read the text to confirm their guesses. They may also develop a framework with which to remember the new words.

Procedure

1. Select 20–30 vocabulary items from a reading selection (fewer for beginning-level students). Select words that are globally related to one or two different characters (e.g., *Pocahontas* and *Capt. John Smith*), one of two different groups (e.g., *whales* and *Eskimos*), or one of two different situations (e.g., *the Iron Age* and *the Modern Age*).

2. Divide a large sheet of chart paper into two equal parts and label each side with the appropriate heading:

Pocahontas	*Capt. John Smith*

3. Divide students into groups (2–4 per group) and give each group a chart and a packet of vocabulary cards.

4. Divide the vocabulary cards so that all students have an equal number. Tell students to place each vocabulary card under the title to which they think it refers. For example:

Pocahontas	*Capt. John Smith*
moccasins	sailor
princess	bearded
Wampanoag	English

All students in the group must reach a consensus on the placement before the vocabulary card is placed on the chart.

5. After the sorting, ask students to read the story to determine if they have sorted the vocabulary correctly. They may change their vocabulary placement at this time if everyone in the group agrees.

Caveats and Options

Students may sort by two, three, or four categories depending on the structure of the text used.

Contributor

Linda New Levine is an ESL teacher in the Bedford Public Schools, Mount Kisco, New York. She conducts teacher-training workshops for ESL and mainstream teachers.

◆ Comprehension
Teacher's Time Out

Levels
Any

Aims
Encourage general
comprehension as well
as attention to
individual, unfamiliar
words or phrases

Class Time
No set time

Preparation Time
None

Resources
Any reading passage

Students understand more than they think they do and benefit from some encouraged independence. A major aim in the teaching of reading is to get students to use their knowledge to help them with their comprehension of a reading. This activity helps to make students realize that they understand more than they think and that they can use this knowledge while reading. It also encourages them to be independent readers.

Procedure

1. Read the passage aloud, but offer no explanation.
2. After reading, have the students write five questions about the passage:
   - about a word they don't know
   - about a phrase or sentence they don't know
   - about a picture or illustration, if there is one
   - about general meaning
   - about cultural areas they find striking
3. Place the students in groups of four to six and assign different questions to each group.
4. Have each group write its "unanswered" questions on the board.
5. Assign other groups to answer these questions on the board.
6. Clear up any misunderstandings.

Contributor

Valerie Benson is Assistant Professor at Suzugamine Women's College, Hiroshima, Japan. Her research interests include reading and teaching with video.

Newspaper Posters

Levels
Beginning

Aims
Present different
sections of a newspaper
to encourage students
to read it

Class Time
30–40 minutes

Preparation Time
30 minutes

Resources
Articles from
newspapers
Large poster boards
Scissors, glue, and
markers

Understanding the content of the sections in a newspaper is essential for proceeding in a course that uses newspapers extensively. English-language newspapers also give students access to more of the English-speaking world around them. This activity is a great icebreaker at the start of a term.

Procedure

1. Clip an assortment of articles and other items from newspapers. Be sure to include enough items from all parts of the papers for all the groups to have plenty to choose from.
2. Provide a list of all categories to be included in the posters. For example: front page, metro, business, sports, lifestyles, entertainment, classifieds.
3. Put the students into groups. Each group uses a poster board and creates a poster that represents the various items found in the different sections, choosing from the articles and items you provide. Ask the students to label the categories.

Caveats and Options

This activity can be completed in several shorter sessions instead of one long one.

Contributor

Caroline Crolley is a candidate for an MA in ESL at the University of Hawaii, where she also teaches.

Theme Readings

Levels
Intermediate +

Aims
Encourage students to
summarize related
articles

Class Time
1 hour

Preparation Time
None

Resources
Magazines and
newspapers

It is always easier for students to read about something they are interested in or would like to know more about. Having students summarize related articles from newspapers and magazines encourages them to use many of their developing language skills for a real-life task and helps them recycle newly acquired vocabulary.

Procedure

1. Select a theme (e.g., food, weather, soccer) and have students find readings on this theme appropriate to their levels.
2. Ask the students to bring in their reading selection for prior approval if necessary. (This is a good idea in the beginning because the students may not be sure what is expected of them.) For lower-level students, collect appropriate articles and have students choose articles from this collection.
3. Have students orally summarize their articles for the class.
4. If students are nervous about giving an oral explanation, give them a few minutes at the beginning of class to practice their summary with a partner. The actual presentation length can vary from 5 to 15 minutes.
5. Ask students to take notes while their classmates are explaining their readings and encourage them to ask questions if they are not clear about the summary. Do not become too involved with the discussions yourself, or students may become dependent on your carrying the discussion.
6. Have students keep a theme reading notebook of the articles and summaries. Check the accuracy and the quality of the summaries, making comments about their presentations, and if needed, suggestions for improvement.

7. Ask students to choose a vocabulary word from their theme readings to teach to the class. The students should find a word they do not know and think would be useful for the class to know.

8. Have students look up the meaning and write an original sentence with the word in it. Ask them to write the word, meaning, and sentence on the board for the class to copy. (Syllable division and stress can also be included in the presentation of the word. The student can also prepare the word ahead of time on a big piece of paper, which saves time in class.) Inform the class that they are responsible for all the theme reading vocabulary words and that you may later test them.

9. Have each student write a question concerning the theme reading, preferably about a major point in the article. Discuss the question and answer with each student before the presentation.

10. Evaluate a student's work by these three criteria:
    - Clarity of summary and ability to explain the article
    - Appropriateness of article (for the particular theme and for class interest)
    - Appropriateness of vocabulary word

Caveats and Options

1. Some possible themes are family, technology, travel, music. . . . Choose topics appropriate to the makeup of the class.
2. Students may enjoy putting together a native dish cookbook during the lesson with the theme on food.

Contributor

Deborah A. Egan teaches at Interlink Language Center/Guilford College in Greensboro, North Carolina.

Spot the Differences

Levels
Intermediate +

Aims
Practice reading
authentic texts for
details
Increase students'
reading speed

Class Time
50 minutes

Preparation Time
30 minutes

Resources
Two short articles on
the same topic from
different sources

After students are skillful enough to discern main ideas, they need to be able to read for details. Short articles with a few obvious differences in information are a good way to practice simple critical reading skills.

Procedure

1. Locate two articles on the same topic but with some conflicting information (e.g., from a newspaper and a movie magazine).
2. Prepare a set of comprehension questions based on both of the articles. Be sure to include questions for which the answers will conflict depending on the article. Also include questions that can be only answered from reading one of the articles.
3. Give half the class one article and a list of questions and the other half of the class the other article but with the same list of questions.
4. Tell the students to read their article and to answer as many questions as they can.
5. Next, have the students find other students with the other article to get the answers to the missing questions. At this point, require the students to prove their answers are correct by pointing out the information in the article.
6. After all of the questions have been answered, hold a discussion about the conflicting facts.

Caveats and Options

It can be difficult to get two articles about the same thing. Sometimes simply buying two different newspapers will provide you with two different sets of facts. Magazines like the *Enquirer* often offer a second article with an opposing point of view.

Contributor

Kelley M. Fast is an ESL instructor, Department of Applied Language Studies, Brock University, Ontario, Canada.

Going Interactive With Reading

Levels
Intermediate +

Aims
Read for main ideas and
main supporting points
Build students'
confidence in writing
summaries

Class Time
30–40 minutes

Preparations Time
No set time

Resources
SRA Rate Builders or
other timed readings
Articles from *News for
You* or other
newspapers
Articles from *Time* or
Newsweek
Passages from readers
such as *In Context* or
Between the Lines

To communicate clearly with one another about something they've read, students need to work with a text enough to understand at least its main and supporting ideas. This activity asks students to use the whole range of language skills in explaining what they've read to their classmates.

Procedure

Sequence A

1. Divide students into pairs, asking each to select a reading.If you are using rate builders, choose one after students have completed a regular three-card timed reading session. If you are using newspapers, have students skim the paper and choose an article, checking with their partners to be sure they will be reading different articles.
2. After students read their chosen article or passage, have them make a brief outline or diagram, identifying the topic, main idea, and supporting points.
3. Ask students to report on their article or passage to their partners. Partners should listen, ask questions, and take notes if they will be writing a summary.
4. Have either the relaters or listeners write a main idea statement or a summary. Avoid having students refer to the reading. If the listeners write the summaries, the summaries should be checked by the relaters. Another option is to have the listeners read the passages they have heard about and discuss with the relaters any omissions they think significant. With the rate builders or any passages accompanied by comprehension quizzes, still another option is to have the listeners take the quizzes.

Sequence B

1–3. Follow Steps 1–3 of Sequence A.
4. Have students interview their partners silently by writing questions and answers to each other about their respective readings. Prime students with the reporter's question word list (e.g., *who, what, where, when*) to follow in asking the questions. The first would normally be, *What is the topic of your article?*
5. Have interviewers use the written interview to write summaries of their partners' articles or passages.
6. Have students read their partners' readings or passages or read each others' summaries and give feedback. (After getting this input, students may revise their summaries before turning them in.)

References and Further Reading

Zukowski/Faust, J., Johnston, S. S., & Atkinson, C. S. (1983). *Between the lines*. New York: Holt, Rinehart & Winston.

Zukowski/Faust, J., Johnston, S. S., Atkinson, C. S., & Templin, E. (1982). *In context*. New York: Holt, Rinehart & Winston.

Contributor

Charlotte Gilman has taught and done teacher training in the Texas Intensive English Program and in secondary schools in the United States, Hong Kong, Malaysia, and Mexico.

Beyond Jigsaw Reading

Levels
Any

Aims
Practice reading rapidly
for main ideas
Develop reporting/
summarizing skills
Encourage students to
generate their own
questions on a text or
topic

Class Time
30–90 minutes

Preparation Time
1 hour

Resources
Blank game board and
dice
Any reading materials,
linked in theme (at
least three medium-
length passages and
eight short passages)

This activity creates a situation in which students are reading and summarizing quickly but without stress due to the gamelike and group-oriented nature of the activity. It promotes student autonomy and replaces teacher- and text-generated comprehension questions.

Procedure

1. Locate suitable reading materials grouped around a single theme. These can be from the textbook the students use or any supplementary reading materials.
2. Fill in a copy of blank game board (see Appendix below) with three types of instruction, one instruction in each box:
   - Questions on the theme of the longer texts, for example, *Give your opinion on...* or *Does X agree with the idea that Y...*
   - Instructions to players to ask other students in the group a question on a specific topic
   - The instruction *3-minute report* (i.e., the student who lands on this box must go to one of the shorter reading passages pinned up around the room, read for 3 minutes, and then report back to the group on what s/he has read).
3. Pin up the shorter reading passages around the room.
4. Assign groups of three to five students to play on one board, throwing dice to determine their moves. Play continues while students are doing their 3-minute reports.

Caveats and Options

1. Include "free question" boxes on game boards to enable students to ask each other any other questions on the theme or readings.

2. On game boards, include boxes with vocabulary definition questions and allow students to consult a classroom English-English dictionary if necessary.
3. Include "blackboard" comment boxes on game boards so that when a student lands on such a box, s/he must write a comment on the topic or readings on the classroom blackboard.
4. We have used this activity successfully in teacher training as well as in college reading classes. It is truly interactive in terms of student-text and student-student interaction. It provides a useful bridge between reading and discussion.

Appendix: Sample Game Board

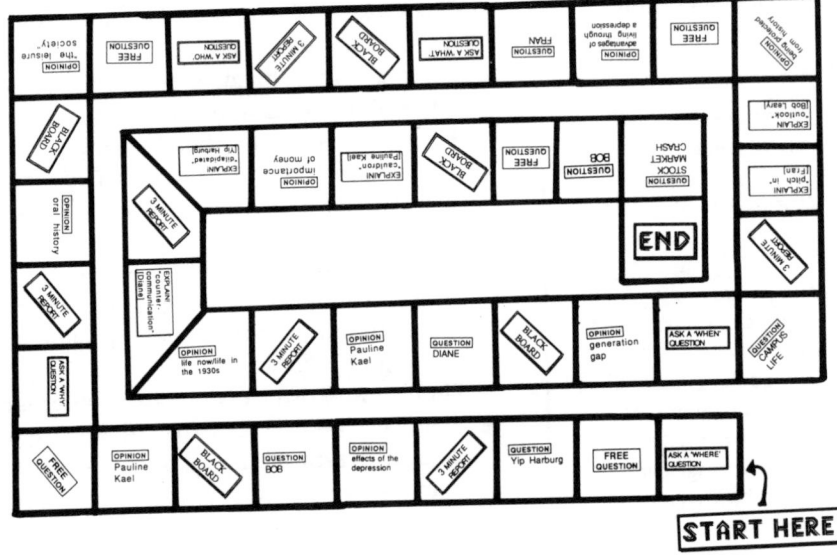

Contributors

Nanci Graves and Sheila Hones teach in the MA Program in TESOL, Columbia University Teachers College, Tokyo, Japan.

The Content and Process Loop

Levels
Advanced; teacher trainees

Aims
Encourage students to respond to content subjectively and objectively as well as to interact with one another

Class Time
2 hours

Preparation Time
1 hour

Resources
Enough desks for four work stations
Three sets of reading passages from Williams (1984)
Several reading texts

This activity encourages teacher trainees to realize that reading can be purposeful and fun and that reading lessons can be settings for meaningful interaction. As they work through passages and tasks, they find out that there can be more than one good response to a question.

Procedure

1. Make enough copies of reading materials for four work stations.
2. Set up four work stations, assigning specific tasks to each one (see below).
3. Direct students to complete the activities at each station.

Work Station 1

1. Ask students to discuss and record as a group whether they agree or disagree with the following statements:
   - You must first be interested in the topic of any reading text to be able to understand the text.
   - You must be able to relate your interests, views, and knowledge to any text you read to be able to understand the text.
   - You must know every single word or structure in a text to understand the text.
2. Ask students to read the passage assigned to the work station and then answer the following questions:
   - What do you think is wrong when a teacher starts a reading lesson with: "Please turn to page 34. Read the passage and answer the questions."
   - What do you think a prereading phase is?
   - Why would you want to include a prereading phase in a reading lesson?

- How can/could visuals (e.g., diagrams, maps, photographs) play a part in prereading?
- Do you think it is important for a teacher to explain all unknown words and structures in the text to students? Why or why not?
- If you want to prepare yourself for prereading, what questions must you ask yourself?

3. Ask students to discuss and record at least three kinds of prereading activities that they feel will be suitable for the passage assigned to the work station.

Work Station 2

1. Ask students to discuss and record the following questions as a group.
   - What are pre-text questions?
   - What is the purpose of the pre-text questions?
   - Are pre-text questions posed at the prereading phase or the while-reading phase? Explain.
2. Ask the group to skim their reading passage and then read it more carefully in order to find answers to accompanying questions.
3. Ask students to discuss
   - why they think completing diagrams or maps, making lists, or taking notes could be considered while-reading activities? Have them come up with three other while-reading activities.
   - if they think it is necessary to read a text first for global understanding and then a second time to answer specific while-reading questions.
   - if they can you provide another label for this phase.
4. Have students review the set of texts provided. They should choose one text to work on as a group, deciding on at least three kinds of while-reading activities they think will be suitable for the text.

Work Station 3

1. Ask students to discuss and record their answers to the questions below:
   - Post-reading can promote interactive work.

- The post-reading phase leads to integration of the skill in a coherent manner.
- The post-reading phase is a compulsory phase to be carried out after every reading.
- Traditional comprehension exercises at the end of a text are a typical post-reading activity.

2. Ask this group to read their assigned passage.
3. Ask the group to discuss and record answers to the following questions:
   - What is the purpose of post-reading work?
   - How is the post-reading activity different from the while-reading type of activity? Give three differences.
   - What must be taken into consideration when a teacher wants to set up and organize post-reading activities?
   - How are questions posed by teachers in preparation for post-reading ideas different from those posed for while-reading ideas?
   - From your own experience, what type of post-reading activities could include interactive work in the classroom?
   - Do you think post-reading work is necessary all the time? Explain.
4. Have students review the set of texts provided. They should choose one text to work on as a group, deciding on at least three kinds of post-reading activities they think will be suitable for the text.

Work Station 4

1. Ask the full class to
   - Reflect on the activities they completed at the work stations.
   - Describe the process they have gone through as a result of participating in the activities so far provided.
   - Jot down what they think and feel the purpose of the process was.
   - State what they have learned about the three-phase approach to reading.

References and Further Reading

Williams, E. W. (1984). *Reading in the language classroom.* England: MacMillan.

Contributors

Bahiyah Bt. Dato' HJ. Abdul Hamid is a lecturer at the Language Centre, Universiti Kebangsaan Malaysia, where she also is the coordinator of the BEd TESL program. Hazita Azman is a lecturer and Deputy Dean at the Language Centre, Universiti Kebangsaan Malaysia.

Mixed Up Comprehension

Levels
Any

Aims
Develop a variety of
reading strategies

Class Time
30–45 minutes

Preparation Time
15–20 minutes

Resources
Passages from students'
reading text or other
sources

Lower-level reading skills such as decoding and graphic cue recognition should be learned along with higher-level reading skills such as applying prior knowledge to the reading passage.

Procedure

1. Make up 5–10 comprehension questions based on the reading passage selected (see Appendix below).
2. Write the comprehension questions on the board or have the questions prepared on a handout.
3. Have students write a reading passage that answers the questions. The students can use their imaginations and write anything, but the passage must be able to answer every question.
4. Read the stories out loud.
5. Compare with original reading.

Appendix: Sample Questions and Passage

1. Why did the country bumpkin go into town?
2. What did his friend look like?
3. How did they return to the country?
4. What did the man do when the horse stopped the first time?
5. What did the man do when the horse stopped the second time?
6. What did the man do when the horse stopped the third time?
7. What did the friend say when the man shot the horse?
8. How did the man reply?

One day a country bumpkin went into town to meet his friend from the city. He finally found his friend waiting for him at the train station. After a quick tour of the city, they began their return to the country in a rented horse and carriage. About an hour down the road the horse came to a stop and wouldn't go on. The country bumpkin became angry and shouted at the horse, "That's one." Finally, the horse started up and they set off down the road again. However, the horse stopped soon after that. Again, the man became angry and yelled at the horse, "That's two." The horse only shook its head and started plodding along. The friends were near their home when the horse stopped for the third time. "That's three," the man said as he pulled out a gun and shot the horse. "Why did you do that?" asked the friend. "That's one," replied the man.

Contributor

Katharine Isbell is the Program Developer and an instructor for the Asahi Chemical Industry Co. employee English program in Nobeoka, Japan. Previously, she was a teacher trainer in Thailand and Indonesia.

Read and Draw

Levels
Any

Aims
Have readers work
cooperatively to share
their knowledge of a
reading passage

Class Time
30–45 minutes

Preparation Time
30 minutes

Resources
Passages from students'
reading text or other
sources

This activity aids comprehension by allowing students to look at the reading from a different point of view. It also encourages the sharing of insights into the article by students.

Procedure

1. Divide the reading passage into five or six easy-to-read parts and write each part on an index card. Make sure the reading is one that lends itself well to drawing and make sure each part has an element in it that can be drawn.
2. Divide the students into as many groups as you have parts of the reading. Explain the activity. Have the students, working together in small groups, read their part of the story and then draw what they have read.
3. Give one piece of paper and a pen to each group. Remember, students should work cooperatively.
4. After each group has drawn their portion of the story, post the drawings.
5. Have a representative from each group explain the drawing.

Caveats and Options

1. Try a reading passage that is not so easy to draw. You'll be surprised at the students' creativity.
2. If you have not done cooperative learning activities in the class before, you might want to introduce the concept of cooperative learning before you try this activity.

References and Further Reading

Burch, R. (1989). *Cooperative learning workshop.* Thai TESOL Convention.

Contributor

Katharine Isbell is the Program Developer and an instructor for the Asahi Chemical Industry Co. employee English program in Nobeoka, Japan. Previously, she was a teacher trainer in Thailand and Indonesia.

Team Comprehension Questions

Levels
Any

Aims
Give students a purpose for reading

Class Time
15–45 minutes

Preparation Time
None

Resources
Passages from students' reading text or other sources

Students use their skimming and scanning skills naturally as they reread passages to find information. This activity is the opposite of the tried-and-true approach to determining the degree of student reading comprehension. having the students generate questions increases motivation. In addition, they use their skimming and scanning skills as they reread the passages to create their questions.

Procedure

1. Have the students read the selected passage.
2. Put the students into small groups and ask each group to develop comprehension questions based on the passage. The number of comprehension questions will depend on the level of the students. The questions can be any type, but each group should be able to answer their own questions.
3. Have the groups share their questions. (This works especially well if the activity is presented as a contest, with points awarded for correct answers.)

Caveats and Options

1. Give different passages to each student.
2. Direct the students to read their passages and to develop comprehension questions on them.
3. When the students have completed the task or the set time limit has expired, tell them to pass the passage and questions to the classmates behind them.
4. Have the latter students read the passage and answer the comprehension questions the former students developed. This alternative works well with the newspaper. Give each student one page of the newspa-

per and ask for comprehension questions on one of the articles. The next student must scan the page to find the article, then skim the article to answer the questions.

Contributor

Katharine Isbell is the Program Developer and an instructor for the Asahi Chemical Industry Co. employee English program in Nobeoka, Japan. Previously, she was a teacher trainer in Thailand and Indonesia.

Getting the Facts Straight

Levels
Intermediate

Aims
Promote the use of
tasks that help readers
sort out, organize, and
retain factual content

Class Time
No set time

Preparation Time
No set time

Resources
Any appropriate reading
passage

There are times when the retention of a large number of ideas or facts is important to one's overall comprehension of a reading assignment or passage. When reading novels, for example, it is easy to be confused by the introduction of many characters early on. Although this is not unique to reading in a foreign language, the added burden makes unnecessarily complex an already difficult task. Requiring readers to work with the ideas or facts while providing a framework with which to organize them can be of great help.

In addition, recent research shows the efficacy of task-based learning. Though tasks can be given both during and after the reading assignment, the two examples below will illustrate their use during reading.

Procedure

Examine any passage your students will read. Figure out how you can create a task from the reading. The two examples below illustrate how this might be done.

1. One semester, my intermediate students were required to read a short novel entitled, *The Best Christmas Pageant Ever*. In addition to a host of characters, both young and old, the plot involves a number of the characters taking on different roles in a church play about the story of Jesus' birth.

   Having just determined who all the characters were, my students also needed to remember who was going to be who in the upcoming play. To lighten the burden, I provided each student with a program (similar to what one might expect to receive from the usher when attending a play or concert), but which was only partially completed (see below). In addition to being nearly realistic, the program gave them a basis for expectation as they read the chapter, and a framework upon which to organize their retention.

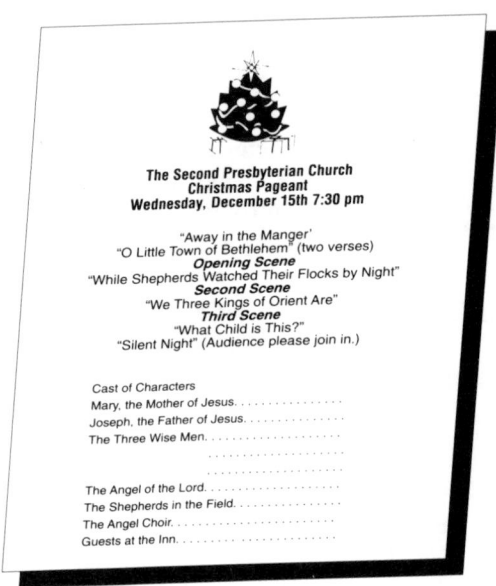

The Second Presbyterian Church
Christmas Pageant
Wednesday, December 15th 7:30 pm

"Away in the Manger'
"O Little Town of Bethlehem" (two verses)
Opening Scene
"While Shepherds Watched Their Flocks by Night"
Second Scene
"We Three Kings of Orient Are"
Third Scene
"What Child is This?"
"Silent Night" (Audience please join in.)

Cast of Characters
Mary, the Mother of Jesus. . . . .
Joseph, the Father of Jesus. . . . .
The Three Wise Men. . . . .
. . . .
. . . .
The Angel of the Lord. . . . .
The Shepherds in the Field. . . . .
The Angel Choir. . . . .
Guests at the Inn. . . . .

2. In intermediate-level reading classes, I sometimes assign an article about the experience of a woman whose apartment was burglarized while she was away on vacation. The author's purpose in writing about her unfortunate experience is to offer readers advice in matters of home security.

The author describes the scene upon her return, the routine investigation, and the resulting visit of a security officer who inspects and evaluates the security of her place. The evaluation covers various areas of concern such as the windows, doors, locks, lighting. As a result of the inspection, the security officer then offers several suggestions. Obviously, these are items for readers to think about, and they result in advice the author thinks we could profit from.

As a way of organizing the information which my students are to gain from this article, I created a mock evaluation form, similar to the one that might have been used by the security officer (see below). Then, as the students read through the article, they fill out the evaluation form item by item, just as the officer might have.

Defense Security Inc.

Name of owner: _____

Type of Dwelling: _____

Item:	Adequate	Not Adequate
1. Front door		
2. Back door		
3. Garage		
4. Sliding doors		
5. Locks		
6. Lighting		
7. Alarm systems		

Recommendations:

From James, M., & Evans, N. (1989). *Beyond words: An advanced ESL reader.* Englewood Cliffs, NJ: Prentice Hall. Chart used with permission.

Contributor

Mark James, a doctoral candidate at the University of Hawaii, is Assistant Director of the TESOL Program at Brigham Young University, Hawaii and co-author of Beyond Words: An Advanced ESL Reader.

Chart Exercise

Levels
High beginning +

Aims
Help students pick out important points in reading passage and see relationships among pieces of information

Class Time
30 minutes

Preparation Time
20 minutes

Resources
A reading passage with two or more parallel sets of information, for example, dates, events, and people involved

Appendix: Sample Chart Exercise

A critical element in comprehension is being able to see relationships among pieces of information in a reading. This activity helps students do this by having them recognize and deal with the same information in a different form.

Procedure

1. Based on the information in the passage, make columns of information, labeled across the top with headings such as date, event, and result, depending on what is appropriate for a particular reading (see Appendix below). Fill in the information in some boxes and leave others blank. (It is not necessary that there be information in every box.)
2. Have students fill in the empty boxes after reading the passage (and perhaps after doing other comprehension exercises).
3. Discuss trends or relationships revealed by the chart, if any.

Caveats and Options

For less advanced students, spaces for which no information is available should be blocked out to indicate the lack of data. The number of spaces left blank depends on the proficiency of the students.

The following is part of a chart exercise from a reading on television in the United States.
Directions: Fill in this chart with types of programs mentioned in the article and a description or examples, if any are given.

Type of Program	Description or Example
1. Serial	
2. _____	
3. _____	
4. _____	
	national and local
5. Cartoon	
6. _____	
7. _____	
8. Movie	
9. _____	
10. _____	
11. _____	"Shogun" and "Roots"
12. Combination comedy and drama	_____
13. Segment involving some issue, followed by discussion	_____

Excerpt from Kitao, K., et al. (1983). *An American sampler*. Reading, MA: Addison-Wesley.

Contributor

S. Kathleen Kitao teaches at Doshisha Women's College in Tanabe, Kyoto, Japan.

Different Perspectives

Levels
Intermediate +

Aims
Sensitize students to
bias in authentic texts

Class Time
30–45 minutes

Preparation Time
45 minutes

Resources
Articles from
newspapers or
magazines

It is important for students to develop an ability to interpret how different texts on the same subject may present particular biases. Although this activity draws its text from the news media, it helps students practice the critical reading skills they need for any sort of purposeful reading.

Procedure

1. Select two newspaper articles of similar length, on the same news item. Make class sets of each article.
2. Put students in pairs and give each student a different article.
3. Have students read their articles individually. Then, without letting them look at each others' texts, ask them to discuss as many factual differences as they can find in the two texts. One of the students should make notes of the differences.
4. Have students reveal their texts to each other and make a further comparative check between the two texts. In addition to looking for factual differences, they should also look for differences in language use and discourse organization. Ask them to note differences.
5. Integrate the student pairs into larger groups of four and have them compare their findings, discussing the different perspectives of each article.

Caveats and Options

1. For lower-level classes, modify the activity: Have students compare two recipes for the same dish from different cookbooks, for example.
2. For more advanced-level students, ask them to compare newspaper editorials or news analyses.
3. With lower-level classes, this activity is a good way to practice intensive reading. With suitable classes at a higher level, it is also a good way of analyzing and interpreting textual bias.

4. The success of this activity depends largely on the choice and matching of suitable and interesting texts.

Contributor

Dino Mahoney is Senior Lecturer at the City Polytechnic of Hong Kong, where, among other things, he is involved with language proficiency course design.

Student's Choice

Levels
High intermediate +

Aims
Involve students in
finding high interest
readings for class use
Vocabulary
development

Class Time
30 minutes

Preparation Time
30 minutes, for students
10 minutes per article,
for teachers

Resources
One-page articles or
selections from
newspapers, magazines,
or other sources

Student motivation and interest are greatly enhanced when reading selections are made by students themselves, when discussion of a reading is student-led, and when the student leader of a group is the source of vocabulary knowledge and the expert on the article.

Procedure

1. Assign students the task of finding a short reading passage that interests them and that they believe will interest classmates. This may be a complete article, or part of one, but should not be longer than one page. Have them clip or photocopy the article and, on a separate sheet, list any words or phrases they find difficult, together with dictionary definitions of the words. Ask for copies of the reading selections and word lists. (See Appendix below.)

2. Add two or three comprehension or discussion questions to the articles. These may be specific to the article or a standard set of questions for all articles (e.g., *What is the main idea? What are the supporting ideas? Why did the author write this?*). Make copies of the articles that will be used in class. There should be enough copies for several groups of students with three or four students in each group. Give each group a different reading passage. Students who choose articles to be used on a particular day should be told in advance when they will be read in class so that they can review the article and its vocabulary in preparation for leading small-group discussion.

3. Divide the students into groups of three or four and distribute the reading passages. Put the students who selected specific readings in the groups that will read their selection; they act as the discussion

leaders and vocabulary consultants. Give the groups about 15 minutes to read and discuss their articles in small groups.

4. After the small-group reading and discussion, ask each group to report to the whole class the gist of its article and some of the comments made by group members during small group discussion.

Caveats and Options

1. It is possible to use student-selected articles for the whole class, thus avoiding group work. In this case, use only one reading at a time with enough copies for the whole class.

2. You may choose to focus on certain themes or genres. For example, the students can be directed to choose passages from newspapers only or from introductory textbooks in their academic fields.

References and Further Reading

Menasche, L. (1985, January). Student's choice: Short readings for the ESL classroom. *English Teaching Forum*, pp. 42–44. (The idea of adding group work was suggested by Mary Connerty, English Language Institute, University of Pittsburgh.)

Appendix: Student's Choice Assignment

Directions: One of our activities this term will be to read and discuss short passages chosen by members of the class.

Homework

1. Find a reading passage that is interesting to you and that you think will be interesting to other students in the class. It must be no longer than one page. The passage can be from any source: newspapers, magazines, books, textbooks, plays, advertisements, catalogues, fiction, nonfiction.

2. Make a copy of the passage (or clip it if it is from a throw-away source such as a newspaper or catalogue).

3. On a separate sheet, make a list of some of the difficult words in the passage and write the dictionary definition next to each word. If the word has more than one definition, be sure to choose the one that fits the use of the word in this passage. (Write your list very clearly so that it can be copied later for the class discussion.)

4. Hand in the copy of the reading passage and the list of words and definitions.

In Class

We will work in small groups to read and discuss the passages. Each group will have a different reading passage. The person who chose the reading will be the discussion leader of the group.

Contributor

Lionel Menasche teaches in the English Language Institute, University of Pittsburgh, in Pennsylvania.

Getting It All Together

Levels
High intermediate +

Aims
Encourage learners to
develop autonomous
reading strategies
Increase students'
awareness of global
concerns

Class Time
50–60 minutes

Preparation Time
30 minutes

Research shows that effective readers check their understanding as they read by asking themselves questions. As students become more proficient at this comprehension monitoring strategy, they become more autonomous, more efficient readers. Because this activity draws from reading materials on global issues, students are monitoring their comprehension (in English) of issues with which they may already be familiar. The result? More motivation, less stress.

Procedures

Reading and Strategy Training

1. Select an appropriate reading passage that is concerned with some aspect of global issues.
2. Prepare questions on the passage and insert them in the passage immediately after the paragraph containing the answer.
3. Prepare a series of discussion questions (see Appendix below) to be used in the critical reading activity.
4. Prepare a comprehension quiz.
5. Have the students read the passage silently. As they read, have them answer the inserted questions aloud or in writing.
6. Immediately after reading, give students the comprehension quiz. Give the answers to the quiz during the Critical Reading Activity.

Critical Reading Activity

1. Work through the discussion questions with students. Make sure they can support their answers by identifying where in the passage they found their them.

2. When the paragraph being discussed contains the answer to a question on the comprehension quiz, refer students to the questions and ask for the answer.

Caveats and Options

1. In order to help students become aware of the strategy of comprehension monitoring, ask them how they feel about reading a text with inserted questions. Point out that research shows that effective readers check their understanding as they read by asking themselves questions such as these.
2. Suggest that students keep a double-entry journal. As they read a passage, they record their responses to it in their journals. In the first column, they copy the word(s), phrase(s), or sentence(s) in the article that trigger responses as they read. In the second column, they write their responses—questions, associations, critical or evaluative responses—anything that crosses their minds as they read. You may collect the journals and select responses for students to write on the board. Repeated modeling and discussion of responses of various types will help students to respond more actively to texts.
3. While doing the critical reading activity, you may wish to list other terms on the board, such as restatement, evidence, claim, assertion, and assumption. Vocabulary unfamiliar to the students may also be listed.

Appendix: Sample Discussion Questions

1. What type of writing is this: narrative, descriptive, expository, argument/position, or literary? How do you know?
2. What controversial issue is dealt with in the passage?
3. Does the author mention an argument against his position? How does the author deal with this possible argument?
4. Is what the author says in the last sentence, Paragraph X, a fact, an opinion, or an informed judgment?
5. In Paragraph Y, Sentence A, why do you think the author used the word _____ ? What effect does this word have on you? Do you read this sentence as a fact or an opinion? Why?
6. In Paragraph Z, Sentence B, why is the word *apparently* used?

7. In Paragraph M, do you agree with the author's proposal? Why or why not?

Contributor

Sylvia Mulling teaches ESL at Kean College. She has extensive teaching and teacher-training experience in Puerto Rico, Algeria, and China, and is a TESOL delegate to the United Nations.

Using Think-Alouds to Teach Reading Strategies

Levels
Any

Aims
Encourage students to use reading strategies to improve reading comprehension

Class Time
50 minutes

Preparation Time
20 minutes

Resources
Any suitable reading material

Effective, efficient reading requires the active participation of the reader. Using think-alouds to teach reading strategies, such as questioning oneself as one reads, provides students with a process-oriented, interactive model of appropriate reading behaviors.

Procedure

1. Choose a suitable text for modeling the strategy. (Make student copies and a transparency.)
2. Explain the strategy to students (i.e., what it is and why good readers use it).
3. Using an overhead transparency of the chosen text, read aloud the first one or two paragraphs of the text while the students listen. While reading, think aloud by telling your listeners what you are thinking, as it relates to the strategy. For example:

   In many countries, such as France, Greece, and Japan, it is often more difficult for students to pass the college entrance exams than to do the course work when they are actually in college, *[How can that be true? Do I understand this correctly?]* and students who don't have much money are at a disadvantage. *[Why are these students at a disadvantage?]* Students prepare for these tests for years in advance. Often, students attend a private school at night (for instance, a *juku* in Japan or a *frontisirion* in Greece) *[So, I guess a juku and a frontisirion are examples of private schools]* to get ready for them. . . .
4. Ask the students to identify the places in the text where you used the strategy. Mark the transparency as students respond.

5. Have students finish reading the article on their own, encouraging them to use the strategy when needed.
6. The next class period, model the strategy again while students mark the text with a symbol assigned to the strategy.
7. Have students compare their answers with those of a partner, then have the entire class discuss the usage of the strategy (where and why).
8. During the third class period, have students practice the strategy individually. Ask them to read a text, mark it with the symbol whenever they use that strategy, and when finished, compare their strategies with a partner.
9. At the end of each class period, have students review the strategy, reiterating what it is, when to use it, and why good readers use it.

Caveats and Options

1. You may model other strategies, for example, predicting, using background knowledge, accepting ambiguities and reading on, searching for connections in the text, and reading selectively. With each new strategy, you should continue to reinforce strategies you have already covered.
2. This activity is based on the belief that in addition to telling students what to do, teachers must also show them how to do it. Therefore, teachers must model processing behaviors rather than simply explain procedural steps.

Contributors

Robert Pritchard is Associate Professor of Education at California State University, Fresno. He holds a PhD in reading/second language learning from Indiana University. Patricia Van Vleet is a full-time ESL instructor at Fresno City College. Her interests are oral communication, pronunciation, and reading strategy research.

Monitoring Comprehension

Levels
Any

Aims
Help students monitor
their comprehension
while reading

Class Time
30–45 minutes

Preparation Time
1 hour

Resources
Article with long,
descriptive paragraphs

Comprehension monitoring allows students to evaluate how well they are reading while they are engaged in doing it. This activity allows students to reflect on their understanding of the article at different stages, predicting what may come next and drawing on previous cultural and personal experience, all of which help in detecting comprehension.

Procedure

1. Using the article you have selected, prepare questions for each paragraph that the students have to answer:
   - Ask readers to reflect on what may have happened in a previous paragraph, predict what may come next, and draw on previous cultural and personal experience.
   - Include some questions specifically about monitoring, in addition to the questions about comprehension, for example: *When you ran into a difficult word or meaning, what did you do? Did you reread the word? read ahead hoping to find the answer? look in a dictionary? ask someone else?*
2. Cut the reading passage into paragraph pieces that you can tape in different places around the classroom in random order.
3. Group the students and send them around the classroom together, with each group starting at a different location.
4. Have students read the paragraph at each location and then answer the questions.
5. Encourage students to work together and answer the questions as a group. They should discuss how they understood the text in order to answer the questions about comprehension and monitoring.
6. Have each group piece together the reading text in the correct order.

7. A general discussion at the end may focus on the main ideas, how students felt as they read each paragraph, and what strategies they used to figure out the paragraph order.

Caveats and Options

After each paragraph, insert a clue, rather than a question, to find the next paragraph. Clues could include pieces from the next or last paragraph.

Contributor

Tee Swan has taught ESL in China and at the University of Hawaii.

Monitoring Text Design

Levels
Intermediate +

Aims
Enable students to
develop strategies for
recognizing and
repairing lagging
comprehension

Class Time
50 minutes

Preparation Time
15–20 minutes

Resources
One or two textbook
sections or magazine
articles

Think-aloud strategies encourage students to assume control of comprehension monitoring. By learning to concentrate on theme, organization, and signal words, students can retrace their steps and figure out where break-downs in their comprehension occur.

Procedure

1. Locate a suitable reading text and bring a class set to the lesson.
2. Give students time to read through the passage silently, then think aloud your procedure for comprehending the passage, highlighting difficult or ambiguous text. Return to unwieldy text as necessary.
3. Talk aloud from the beginning of the passage, predicting thematic focus in the text from the title of the passage.
4. Look for initial, within-body, and final mentions of thematic focus, highlighting key words and ideas.
5. Note text sections with potentially important changes in the controlling idea.
6. Try to identify any predominant rhetorical clustering of information such as process descriptions presented as sequences, comparisons or contrasts presented as hierarchies or matrices, or even cause-effect or problem-solution patterns.
7. Actively search for combinations of patterns or incomplete patterns.
8. Describe the textual signals that you noted, such as the introduction, conclusion, and headings as cues for repairing misunderstood text.
9. Ask one or a pair of the more proficient students to model these monitoring strategies on a different passage. As students work repeatedly on this think-aloud procedure, their remarks will become more refined approximations of their thinking and understanding of text design.

References and Further Reading

Calfee, R. C., & Chambliss, M. J. (1987). The structural design features of large texts. *Educational Psychologist, 22,* 357–378.

Varghese, S. A. (1992). Helping students use text to monitor their comprehension. In A. Kwan-Terry & P. Bodycott (Eds.), *Reading and writing in a multi-cultural society.* Singapore: Society for Reading and Literacy.

Contributor

Susheela A. Varghese teaches theories of reading and writing in the Department of English Language and Literature at the National University of Singapore. She publishes and presents on reading comprehension theory and instruction.

The Art of Reading Comprehension

Levels
Intermediate +

Aims
Help students
understand vocabulary
in context
Encourage students to
monitor their own
comprehension

Class Time
1–2 hours

Preparation Time
1–2 hours

Resources
Any appropriate text
Illustrations from art
books

This technique requires the reader to apply meaning from the text to the actual content to which it refers. The correct responses are pictures, not further text. This means that it is impossible to choose a correct response simply on the basis of linguistic cues. It also is particularly stimulating for those students who are visually (rather than print) oriented in terms of learning style.

Procedure

1. Choose a text that describes an artistic tradition, find illustrations, and make reading questions.
2. Using pictures, preteach key vocabulary, for example: *landscape, scenery, brushstroke, figure, portrait, still-life.*
3. Arrange a number of reproductions of Chinese paintings in random order, for example, along the chalkboard ledge.
4. Ask hypothesis questions, for example, *Which paintings do you think are oldest? Latest?*
5. Read introductory paragraph together, finding examples of vocabulary words in the paintings.
6. Have students read the entire passage (see Appendix below).
7. Ask students to match pictures with the dynasty, stating reasons supported by the text. Which of these pictures could have been painted by Yen Li-Pen? By Han Kan? Why do you think so? Ask students to identify dynasty, style, and artists based on information in the text.

Caveats and Options

1. Use any sequence in an artistic tradition, for example, from French late classical to Impressionists and early Post-Impressionists. This can

also be done horizontally, with different contemporaneous styles, for example, to identify African tribal or regional styles.

2. Chinese students may recognize the paintings, artists and dynasties, but not know the English vocabulary. The assignment can be revised for them to start with the paintings, and then find appropriate descriptive language in the text.

Appendix: Sample Excerpt

The T'ang dynasty (618–906 A.D.) saw the rise of the great art of Chinese landscape painting. . . . Jutting peaks, reaching into the sky, were carefully detailed with trees, rocks, and streams in brilliant greens and blues. Virtually nothing now remains of the work of such famous masters of this period as Yen Li-Pen, Wu Tao-tzu, Tung Yuan, and Wang Wei. During this same period, figure painting, especially of historical and courtly scenes, reached a peak of excellence. People were portrayed with a strength and magnificence unequaled in later Chinese painting. Animals were also frequent subjects during this time. Han Kan, the 8th century artist, is particularly famous for his paintings of horses. Although stylized, made with only a few brushstrokes, their simple strong lines have great energy.

Sharply diminished in scale, the human figure did not intrude upon the magnificence of nature.

Zen Buddhists' paintings were often sparked by an intuitive vision; with rapid brushstrokes and ink splashes, they created works of vigor and spontaneity.

Many landscapes of this period are misty and dream-like; they seem calm and even sad, or constantly shifting and changing.

Excerpt adapted from Harris, W. H., & Levey, J. S. (1975). *The new columbia encyclopedia*. New York: Columbia University Press.

Contributor

Lise Winer teaches in the Applied Linguistics and TESOL programs, Department of Linguistics, Southern Illinois University, and is the author of several ESL readers.

Steppingstones to Reading Instruction

Levels
Intermediate +;
secondary ESL

Aims
Encourage and develop
correct inferences in
reading

Class Time
10 seconds +

Preparation Time
None

Resources
Any reading text

Students, especially those who are unaccustomed to interactive classrooms, are often reluctant to respond to inference questions during class discussion, either because they lack confidence and do not want to risk embarrassment, or because they are unsure of the answer and require additional information in order to shape their realization of a concept or idea. Teachers can encourage and facilitate responses in both instances by offering students hints and choices. These serve as steppingstones that enable students to advance toward a correct inference.

Procedure

1. Focus on a small portion of text. This example uses an excerpt from Lewis Carroll's poem "Jabberwocky":
   Beware the Jabberwock, my son!
   The jaws that bite, the claws that catch!
2. Pose the comprehension-inference question, for example, *What is a Jabberwock?* (The desired answer is anything like "a fierce dangerous animal.")
3. If students do not respond, give a hint or a choice. Often, one such steppingstone will be sufficient, but you can put as many steppingstones as necessary to help students come up with the right answer and vocabulary.

   Hints include the use of leading questions, statements, and nonverbal cues that can move ahead of student development to help shape a correct inference. Nonverbal cues, such as gestures, facial expressions, and sounds can also often expedite a realization. Examples:

- Leading question: *Would you like to have one in your house? Do people have claws?*
- Statement: *It's some kind of animal.*
- Nonverbal hint: *claw the air threateningly, make a fierce face, roar*

Especially recommended are leading questions with obvious negative answers, such as *Would you like to have one in your house?* which evoke laughter and comic protest. Nonverbal hints also tend to evoke laughter and lower affective barriers.

Choices involve the presentation of possible answers, usually in pairs. A choice may include: (a) one very likely possible choice and one very unlikely choice; (b) two highly unlikely choices; (c) two likely choices:

a. Is it friendly or unfriendly? a good thing or a dangerous thing?
b. Is it a mouse or a butterfly?
c. Is it an animal or a demon?

Especially recommended is choice type a. An unlikely choice, when paired with a likely choice, is usually obvious to the students and evokes laughter or smiles of rejection. This gives students a chance to make a very safe choice, and get credit for moving along the path to the right answer.

References and Further Reading

Carroll, L. (1971 [1872]). Jabberwocky. In *Through the looking glass.* Harmondsworth, England: Penguin.

Contributors

Lise Winer teaches in the Applied Linguistics and TESOL programs, Department of Linguistics, Southern Illinois University, and is the author of several ESL readers. Scott Benson is a graduate of the MA in EFL program at Southern Illinois University-Carbondale. He is currently teaching English in Saudi Arabia.

◆ Main Ideas
Do-It-Yourself Materials

Levels
Lower intermediate +

Aims
Practice reading
authentic texts

Class Time
20 minutes

Preparation Time
30 minutes

Resources
Brochures from
supermarkets,
department stores,
government agencies,
political groups

Students need to be able to make sense of public information resources independently. This activity uses brochures on any number of topics that might be of interest or use to them.

Procedure

1. Locate suitable brochures. If your class is interested in current events, you might use an informational pamphlet from a group such as Amnesty International. Alternatively, you can find informational pamphlets about food at the supermarket or those relating to health issues through doctors' offices or public agencies.
2. Most brochures follow a question-and-answer format (e.g., *What is Amnesty International?*) or make extensive use of headlines and subtitles (e.g., *Garlic and Health*). Separate the questions, headlines, or titles from the paragraphs they match.
3. Think up a preview question, getting the students to focus on the topic (*What do you know about X? What would you like to know? What kinds of things would you like to know about an organization before you joined it?*). Get answers from the whole class.
4. Put the students in groups and ask them to match the titles and paragraphs.
5. As a comprehension check, ask the students, in groups, to list two or three facts they learned about the topic.

Contributor

Steven Brown is on the staff of the University of Pittsburgh English Language Institute in Pennsylvania. He is a co-author of the English Firsthand *and* English Firsthand Beginners' Course *text series.*

What's in the News?

Levels
Intermediate +

Aims
Practice reading
authentic texts from
newspapers

Class Time
50 minutes

Preparation Time
20 minutes

Resources
Short articles from
English-language
newspapers

Recognizing the main idea and themes in newspaper articles helps readers process and retain information on current events. Reading authentic articles also gives learners appropriate background knowledge for related class projects.

Procedure

1. Ask each student to bring an article from an English language newspaper on a common topic (e.g., crime, pollution, accidents).
2. In class, put students in groups of three or four and have them retell their information, classifying it into specific categories (e.g., homicide, robbery, assault).
3. Next, have students walk around the room and find out who else has articles that match their own categories.
4. After groups with similar categories are formed, direct a whole-class discussion to make a list of all the categories on the board. Students can contribute additional information from their own experiences.
5. Post-reading activities requiring writing can be assigned, such as summaries, letters to government officials offering suggestions to deal with problems, and responses in journals.

Contributor

Millie Commander is Associate Professor of English and Linguistics at Inter American University, Puerto Rico. She teaches ESL reading to undergraduates and ESL methodology courses to graduate students. She received a PhD in TESOL from New York University.

Piecing Together Ideas

Levels
Intermediate +

Aims
Practice reading for
main ideas
Develop skill in reading
for details

Class Time
20–30 minutes

Preparation Time
No set time

Resources
Any reading material
Paper
Hat

Making distinctions between general ideas and supporting details is an important part of reading comprehension. Strip stories are an enjoyable way for students to see the relationship between the bigger and smaller pieces of a text.

Procedure

1. Select appropriate reading material for the class.
2. Select sentences or paraphrase portions of the reading passage and write them on strips of paper. Prepare a set of corresponding strips that say either "main idea" or "supporting detail." The two sets of strips must correspond exactly. The total number of strips should equal the number of students in the class.
3. As the students read the material, devote class time to enhancing comprehension until the material is well understood.
4. Have students
   - draw a strip from a hat.
   - work together to match the strips with the quotations to the strips with the labels.
   - stand in a line (with a strip) in the order that the sentences appeared in the reading passage.
   - read out loud, in sequence, what is written on the individual strip.

Caveats and Options

1. For a large class, use two sets of strips and have two groups form two different lines simultaneously.
2. Make the activity more difficult by requiring any reading material to be put away before the strips are drawn from the hat so students may not refer to it during the exercise.
3. It is important to have covered the material well before attempting this activity, but it is a nice way to conclude work on a reading passage.

Contributor

Caroline Crolley is a candidate for an MA in ESL at the University of Hawaii, where she also teaches.

Recreate the Caption

Levels
Intermediate +

Aims
Practice recognizing
main ideas in
newspaper or academic
articles
Create a graphic
representation of main
ideas

Class Time
30–40 minutes

Preparation Time
30 minutes

Resources
Articles from
newspapers or
textbooks, accompanied
by charts, graphs,
information diagrams,
or illustrations

Important ideas in the newspaper or in academic articles are often presented in both words and illustration. If students understand the main ideas in a text, they should be able to identify the representation of the ideas in graphic form. This activity asks students to use their understanding to supply missing pieces of information.

Procedure

1. Locate appropriate articles of 10–12 paragraphs, illustrated with suitable diagrams. Make enough copies for each student.
2. Remove key captions or text information from any illustrations, diagrams, charts or graphs.
3. Create groups of four students. Distribute the article and diagrams. Have the students read the article carefully and then try to recreate the missing captions or other text with their group.
4. Ask groups to record their possible captions or labels and then share them with the class.
5. Reveal the actual captions or labels and have the class discuss how their answers differed.

Caveats and Options

This activity can also be done with more advanced classes using chapters from academic textbooks as part of a unit on a particular theme. As students read the chapter, repeat the procedure above using diagrams from the chapter, having students recreate the captions, titles, or labels.

Contributors

Debbie Davis is Assistant Director of the ESL program at California State University (CSU) at Fresno and also an instructor. Ellen Lipp teaches linguistics at CSU and directs the ESL program.

Match the Headline

Levels
Intermediate +

Aims
Practice reading for
main ideas in magazines
and newspapers

Class Time
30 minutes

Preparation Time
30 minutes

Resources
Short news articles with
headings

Matching headlines with articles helps students better understand the point of a reading. Using authentic materials often increases student interest and motivation.

Procedure

1. Locate suitable articles or items from newspapers, of one or two paragraphs in length. Each should have a heading. You will need one article and one heading for each student.
2. Remove the headings from the articles.
3. Create groups of three to four students. Distribute the articles and headings and ask the students to try to match them. Each group will have three or four articles plus headings.
4. Groups should note their suggested matchings, exchange their suggested headings and articles, and continue matching.

Caveats and Options

1. Add further headings to serve as distracters.
2. This activity is best used to practice, not to introduce, the skill. The first time it is used might require some modeling.

Contributor

Richard R. Day, whose early EFL experiences include the Peace Corps in Ethiopia, is Professor of ESL, University of Hawaii.

Up Against the Wall

Levels
Any

Aims
Practice reading for
main ideas

Class Time
Varies, depending on
length of reading
passage

Preparation Time
50 minutes

Resources
Suitable reading passage

In addition to helping students understand the main ideas of a reading, this activity generates a great deal of excitement and enthusiasm as students get away from their desks and move around the room searching for answers to their questions.

Procedure

1. Make up one question for each main idea of the reading passage. For beginning classes, these can be true/false, cloze with a choice, or multiple choice. For more fluent readers, the questions can be open-ended (e.g., *what, where,* and so on). Duplicate the questions so that every two students in the class will have one question.
2. Cut the passage into sections according to its paragraphs. Fasten the paragraphs to the walls of the classroom, making sure that each paragraph can be read easily by several people at the same time.
3. Place the students in pairs, and give each pair one question. (Depending on the size of the class, any number of pairs will have the same question.) Instruct the students to read the paragraphs on the walls of the classroom until they find the answer to their question.
4. When they have returned to their seats, distribute copies of the complete reading passage and go over the answers. You might also want to pass out copies of all of the questions, making it easier for everyone to understand other groups' questions.

Caveats and Options

1. For more proficient readers, use questions that require students to make inferences.
2. Again, with more proficient readers, ask a question that cannot be answered by reading the passage.

3. To encourage more group work, have pairs with the same question discuss their answers before Step 4 above.
4. Use the activity as a prereading task.

Contributor

Richard R. Day, whose early EFL experiences include the Peace Corps in Ethiopia, is Professor of ESL, University of Hawaii.

Keeping an Eye on the Essentials

Levels
Any

Aims
Practice differentiating essential information from less important information
Practice organizing that essential information in order to convey it to someone else

Class Time
30 minutes–1 hour

Preparation Time
30 minutes–1 hour

Resources
Two short reading passages

Second language readers need to discover that not all words and sentences in a piece of reading deserve equal time and effort. By learning to recognize the essential information, students can read more efficiently. By organizing the information in their minds they can remember it and become more proficient in articulating it.

Procedure

1. Give one article to half the students and the other article to the other half. Ask them to read their articles and be prepared to tell a classmate the important information.
2. In the next class, pair each student with someone who has read the other article. Have students explain to their partners the essential information from their own articles without looking at the article itself (but using any brief notes they may have made). The listeners should ask questions for clarification or more explanation whenever necessary, with the aim of remembering the information presented by their partners.
3. When all students have finished, have them put away all articles and notes and take out a clean piece of paper. Write on the board several basic questions for each article that focus on what you consider to be the essential information. The first question should be *What was the main idea of your partner's reading?*
4. After allowing time for students to write their answers, tell them they can refer briefly to both articles if they need to improve their answers. Give them a little revision time.

5. Go over the answers to the questions. There will be many possible ways to phrase the answers. It will help students to have one sample answer to each question written on the board.

Caveats and Options

1. Putting a time limit on Steps 2–4 encourages preparation and concentrated, efficient communication.
2. Students' written answers to the questions can serve as notes for subsequent oral or written summaries of the articles.
3. In classes where homework is not assigned, do the initial reading in class as well if the articles are short. After the exercise, offer students copies of the articles they did not receive.

Contributor

Nancy Whisler Mutoh received an MA in ESL from the University of Hawaii. She is a permanent faculty member at the Nagoya University of Foreign Studies, Nagoya, Japan.

Getting the Idea

Levels
Intermediate +

Aims
Reduce student
dependency on a
dictionary
Encourage student
acceptance of
uncertainty
Discourage excessive
concern over the
meaning of every word
in a passage
Cultivate the habit of
general reading in
English

Class Time
50 minutes

Preparation Time
20 minutes

Resources
Any reading passage

A text does not always require a careful reading but even when it does, focusing on overall meaning accelerates and enhances comprehension. Students need to discover for themselves the degree to which they are able to derive meaning from a text without understanding (or, in this case, actually seeing) every word in it. Such a discovery works toward promoting a general interest in reading in English.

Procedure

1. Select a suitable passage and give it a title or heading if necessary. Replace main ideas with blank spaces (see Appendix below).
2. Divide the class into groups of four or five students and provide each student with a copy of the doctored passage.
3. Ask the students, working in groups, to examine the passage, discuss it, and then write group summaries of what they think the main idea(s) are.
4. Allow approximately 10 minutes for the students to complete the task, then collect the summaries and all copies of the text.
5. Provide each student with an undoctored copy of the passage. While the groups read it and then write a second summary, copy the collected summaries on the board.
6. Ask a student from each group to come to the board and copy the group's new summary beneath the old one.
7. Ask the class as a whole to identify any differences, if any, between the summaries in each set and to discuss their significance. For example, do any changes in the second summary really add to an understanding of the main idea of the passage?
8. Have the class as a whole analyze all the groups' summaries in terms of any differences. Bring into this analysis the part played by the

title in identifying the main idea of the passage. From this general discussion, the class should arrive at a summary acceptable to all participants.

9. Round off the exercise with a look at any unfamiliar words. Check if students have correctly inferred their meanings. Prompt further inference from context. Explain any words that remain elusive. Finally, ask the students to decide whether their understanding of these words changes the gist of the text.

Caveats and Options

1. The whole or general meaning is contained in the parts of the passage the students first see and in the title, so the deleted words may provide details. Students can see, however, that they have little or no impact on the general meaning.

2. Without the frantic pursuit of word-to-word understanding implicit in intensive reading, students gain the confidence to employ the inference and prediction skills they have already learned and to accept uncertainty as normal.

Appendix: Sample Reading Passage

The Beach Gets a New Look

The next generation will exclaim in amazement, "Imagine, in the olden days people used to actually lie in the sun to get a tan! **Rapidly coming to an end are the days of beaches** rainbow-hued with scattered gaudy towels and glistening **with shiny, oily bodies** that from a distance look like so much flotsam and jetsam washed up with the tide. The **era of sunless tanning is upon us** as manufacturers of sun-care products compete for the new market of consumers educated to the **risks of skin cancer.** Combined with the health fear is the temptation of a **safe, fast tan** that, fake as it may be, is a far cry from the streaky-carrot look that was a give-away in the past. Now the bottle-bronzed blend with the more traditional tanners to form the community of Sybarites crowding pool and beach as the temperature rises.

Advanced technology has allowed the development of a wide range of these new and improved sunless tanning products. Costs vary, but they are all basically the same. As with their predecessors, the active ingredient is DHA (dihydroxy-acetone), but the **new products spread more evenly**

and produce a more natural-looking tan in two to three hours. Since the tan gradually fades in a few days, **repeated applications are necessary** to maintain that much sought after summer-glow. Needless to say such a **booming market** has manufacturers smiling.

Advanced technology is not, however, leaving the stubborn hanging out to dry in the sun unprotected. For those who cannot break their addiction to the sun's deadly embrace, a **new patch** has joined the rush of patches with which we can now adorn our bodies. As harmful exposure to **ultraviolet rays** rises, the patch **changes color to warn** the inveterate **sunbather** of imminent **danger.**

So what will **beaches of the future** look like? Probably another colorful sea, but this time of **shimmering parasols** floating three or four feet above the sand with the sunlessly tanned huddled in their shade for protection. Anomalous squares of open sand harboring the **patched dissenters** will stand out like fragile islands bracing for the onslaught of a tidal wave.

Note: The parts in bold are all that students see at first.

Contributor

Margaret Shabka is Director of the English Language Program at the University of Maryland, Baltimore County. She received her PhD from Kent State University, has taught in six countries, and has published on ESOL writing and literature for second language learners. Her other interests include cross-cultural communication and teaching methodology.

Choosing a Different Title

Levels
High beginning +

Aims
Give students practice
in distinguishing
between main and
supporting ideas

Class Time
20–25 minutes

Preparation Time
5 minutes

Resources
Short news article

This activity is a good way of getting students to realize that authors have many options to choose from in selecting a title and that the actual title used will reflect the taste or bias of the author or editor of the newspaper or magazine in which the article appears.

Procedure

1. Locate a suitable article from a newspaper or magazine. The article should have a title and be about 250–350 words long. Prepare a list of 10 other titles for the article, 5 "good" titles (i.e., titles focusing on the main idea of the article) and 5 "wrong" ones (i.e., distracters focusing on supporting details). You will need one copy of the article and one list of titles for each student.
2. Distribute the article and the list of titles. Divide the class into pairs.
3. Tell the students that they are to read the title of the article and the article itself. Then they are to look at the list of titles and choose 5 more that are also good. They should number the titles from 1 to 5, starting with the one they think is best.
4. Have students work in pairs, choosing and ranking 5 titles.
5. (Optional) Have one student from each pair report to the class.

Caveats and Options

1. As a variation, remove the original title from the article and include it among the titles on the list. Have students guess which title was actually used by the author.
2. As an additional step, ask students to say what is wrong with the other titles in the list.
3. Another option is to have the entire class vote on what they think is the best title for the title.

4. As a follow-up activity or as homework, students can write three to five titles of their own for the article (or some other article).

Contributors

Susan Stempleski, a teacher, teacher trainer, and materials developer, co-authored Explorations, Getting Together, *the* Hello, America *multimedia series, and the award-winning* Video in Action. *Alison Rice, a teacher, teacher trainer, and materials developer, likes activities that involve the learner's intelligence and creativity. Her publications include* Countdown!, Explorations, *and* Getting Together.

◆ Organization and Structure
Who Done It?

Levels
Intermediate

Aims
Practice reading
newspaper articles to
reconstruct a story

Class Time
No set time

Preparation Time
20 minutes

Resources
Newspaper articles
about an event, a
criminal action, a
celebration, or any
activity containing part
of a story

Newspaper articles, especially those related to criminal or police actions, offer students a variety of topics, styles, and levels of difficulty. The information they contain usually includes elements related to time, place, and action. Learners must not only understand the information but be able to reconstruct it chronologically because journalists present the current state of affairs in the opening paragraph and then proceed to narrate the events that led to it.

Procedure

1. Select articles a few paragraphs in length. Long articles can be shortened, but they should contain enough information to make the story coherent.
2. Give the students a copy and ask them to read it.
3. Either write a chart on the board for them to complete, or reproduce it as a handout. Try to have a chart with at least two labels: time and action.
4. As soon as the students have read the article and seen the chart, ask them to fill it in, taking care to organize the information in chronological order, starting either with the most recent time or with the most remote. Have them work individually or in pairs.
5. After a few minutes, when most or all of the students have finished, have them compare their charts.
6. Complete the chart on the board following the directions the students give you. At this stage, it is important to comment on different words used to fill in the chart or on any differences in how students completed it. Reconstructing the story allows students to discuss their different interpretations of it.

7. At this point, the students have all the elements of the story and are ready to narrate it starting from the beginning. Ask them to retell the story or rewrite it.

Contributor

Maria Eugenia Boudeguer is Assistant Professor in the Department of Foreign Languages of the University of Concepción, Chile. She is a teacher of English as well as a translator. She received an MA in Teaching English as a Second Language from the University of Illinois, at Urbana-Champaign.

Note, Organize, Summarize

Levels
Advanced; preacademic

Aims
Encourage active reading and self-monitoring of comprehension

Class Time
Two to three class periods

Preparation Time
45 minutes–1 hour per passage

Resources
Academic textbook-style passages of more than two pages

Students may need help learning to apply reading skills to study techniques when preparing for class discussions, tests, and report writing. They can improve their comprehension if they learn to see how ideas are connected in an entire piece of writing.

Procedure

1. Have the students skim an assigned passage to get a general idea of the content and overall organization. Ask them to discuss the article briefly as a group, then assess how well they have understood the whole passage.
2. Instruct the students to make notes in the margins about important ideas within and across paragraphs. You might model this step with a transparency of the reading and an example of your own notes for the first paragraph or so. One possibility is to give the students a chance to try writing marginal notes about the key ideas for one paragraph and then show them your model or elicit their suggestions.
3. Have students work on their own, making brief marginal notes in their own words of ideas from each paragraph. Special care should be taken to recognize relationships among ideas extending across paragraphs.
4. Divide students into pairs or small groups. Have them compare their marginal notes. After they have made good headway, hand out blank transparencies to each group and have them outline the passage or part of the passage on the transparency.
5. Show outlines from two or more groups, simultaneously if possible. Have students compare similarities and differences with their own group outlines. Encourage questions about why certain points were or were not included in the outline. After discussing the outlines,

have students assess how their comprehension changed from the first, cursory reading to the second reading during which they took their marginal notes.

Caveats and Options

1. Using a student-generated outline, have the students summarize the article orally or in writing. Ask the students not to look at the original while they are summarizing. These summaries can be used to test comprehension.
2. As students become used to this procedure, they can begin writing and comparing their own outlines, instead of notes, with those of their classmates.
3. Semantic maps or other representations of organizational structure may be substituted for outlines.
4. This series of reading activities should be practiced several times throughout a term so that the students begin to acquire independent note-taking strategies.
5. If students are not familiar with outlining or mapping techniques, teachers may have students take marginal notes to fill in partially completed outlines or topic maps. Guidance through the procedure should gradually decrease.
6. Not all passages lend themselves to paragraph-by-paragraph analysis. Students may need some help incorporating ideas from two or more paragraphs into one section of an outline.

Contributors

Marcia Z. Buell and James G. Buell have taught English in Japan, China, the United States and, most recently, Hungary. Their research interests include linking ESL study and testing to academic preparation.

Jigsaw Reading

Levels
Beginning and intermediate

Aims
Help students work cooperatively to figure out the ordering of paragraphs in the reading passage

Class Time
No set time

Preparation Time
20–30 minutes

Resources
Reading passage with at least four paragraphs

This activity has been around for a long time and takes various forms. Regardless of the type of jigsaw reading, the activity is enjoyable and helps students to conceptualize the reading passage by looking at a small part and then fitting the individual pieces together. It works well as a prereading activity.

Procedure

1. Divide the reading passage by paragraphs and make copies for students.
2. Arrange the class into groups according to the number of paragraphs in the reading passage.
3. Give each group a complete set of the passage, making sure that each person has a different paragraph.
4. Tell the students to put the paragraphs together in an appropriate order. Have them begin by reading their own paragraphs and then telling the other members of the group what they are about.
5. Ask the groups to share with the class the ordering that they have agreed on. Discuss the reasons for the various orderings the groups selected.

Caveats and Options

1. Set a time limit—this turns the activity into a contest.
2. For basic readers, do the activity with scrambled sentences instead of paragraphs.
3. Distribute a copy of the original reading passage to each student.

Contributor

Richard R. Day, whose early EFL experiences include the Peace Corps in Ethiopia, is a professor of ESL, University of Hawaii.

Blocking a Reading

Levels
High beginning +

Aims
Practice recognizing
main and supporting
ideas

Class Time
Number of minutes
permitted for reading
plus 15–25 minutes for
discussion

Preparation Time
No set time

Resources
Any article

This effective method for identifying main and major supporting ideas is adaptable to any reading situation and helps make students independent readers. The graphic nature of blocking provides a concrete and tangible sense of the main idea and supporting ideas. Blocking can also be done mentally (after students become familiar with the concept), making it more likely that the students will use this method outside the classroom for independent reading. Finally, the student is weaned from the post-reading comprehension questions offered in reading texts.

Procedure

1. Ask the students, on their first reading, to draw lines in the margin that block out (a) the introduction, (b) each major supporting idea, and (c) the conclusion. Specify a time limit for the reading.
2. Have the students read the article and simultaneously block it.
3. Ask the students to compare and discuss their individual blockings.
4. Lead a class discussion of the students' blockings.

Caveats and Options

If time is lacking, omit Step 3 and go to Step 4.

Contributor

John Holstein received his MA in Linguistics/TESL from Northeastern Illinois University. He has been teaching college-level English in Korea since 1981.

Linking Research Articles to Abstracts

Levels
Intermediate +

Aims
Help students
understand and
recognize the four main
sections of an
experimental research
article
Help students get the
most out of research
article abstracts no
matter how they are
constructed

Class Time
One or more class
periods

Preparation Time
No set time

Resources
At least three authentic
and unadapted abstracts
Overhead projector,
transparencies, pens

Intermediate and advanced students at the university level may not know how to read a professional research article abstract effectively enough to use it as a summary and preview of the full article. For students in the social, biological, and physical sciences, familiarity with the four main sections of an experimental research article—Introduction, Methods and Materials, Results, and Discussion (IMRD)—can aid understanding of the information in any abstract and how it is organized. This activity sensitizes students to the way language creates internal textual boundaries.

Procedure

1. Select and prepare at least three abstracts of experimental research articles. Separate the abstracts from the articles, but retain the titles. One abstract should be organized in the complete IMRD structure. One other abstract should have a nonstandard organization of the four parts, and one should have a missing element or two. Copy these texts onto overhead transparencies, enlarging the text size if you have access to the technology.

2. Introduce or review the four sections of an experimental research article with the class. Have the students (in pairs or groups) brainstorm and pool what sorts of activities they would expect to find in each of the four sections. Write their ideas on the board. For example, for the Introduction, students might come up with hypotheses, basic definitions, or what previous research has not solved. Fill in whatever they leave out.

3. Pass out the complete abstract. Have the students read the text and try to agree on where the boundaries between the four sections are. If relevant, stress that a boundary may even come somewhere inside

a sentence. Tell students to be prepared to explain what language in the text led them to draw the boundaries where they did.

4. Project the abstract on an overhead projector. Have a volunteer come up and draw the boundary markers with a colored pen, labeling the sections with *I*, *M*, *R*, and *D*. Elicit an explanation for the decision.

5. Ask if any other pair or group drew the boundaries differently. If yes, call up a representative from a dissenting pair or group to draw that group's boundary marks and labels with a pen of a different color.

6. Discuss with the class where the two groups agree and disagree on the boundaries and try to come to an explanation for any discrepancy. See if a case can be made for arriving at a consensus. If the discrepancies are well founded, you can exploit them as evidence for variation in certain aspects of the structural analysis of complex texts.

7. Repeat Steps 2–5 with the other abstracts.

Caveats and Options

1. Each round of this activity can be followed by locating in the full article the information given in a particular abstract and by revising the class-created list of expected activities in each section of the experimental research article, based on the sorts of information found in the abstracts.

2. This procedure can be scheduled concurrently with or right after the main sections of the experimental research article have been introduced and several typical full-length research articles have been skimmed.

Contributor

Sally Jacoby has taught courses in and developed materials for ESL/ EFL reading at all levels since 1976.

Sentence-Busting

Levels
Intermediate +; also
false beginners

Aims
Provide a strategy to
help learners attack a
difficult sentence in a
text by deconstructing
it nonlinearly
Raise the consciousness
of learners about how
to decode complex
syntax

Class Time
5–15 minutes

Resources
Any sentence in a larger
text that learners find
insurmountably difficult

ESL/EFL students at any post-beginner level may experience frustration when faced with having to decode and understand what they see as difficult, long, and complex sentences, especially in nonfiction texts. Typically, the frustrated reader will keep returning to the beginning of the sentence and slog through, left to right, trying to make sense in a linear, additive way until giving up. This may even happen when the actual words of the sentence are apparently familiar. In such cases, the difficulty is less a problem of just understanding the words and more one of understanding how the message in the sentence is distributed in the grammar. This activity is based on an approach to difficulty that is rooted in what a learner may already know about English phrase and sentence structure and intersentential cohesion.

Procedure

1. Ask students to find the beginning (the capital letter) and the end (the final punctuation mark) of a whole problematic sentence, even if they understand (or think they understand) part of it. Point out the connection between difficulty and length, if relevant, and what expectations are set up when end punctuation is taken into account.
2. Have the students circle any punctuation inside the sentence and discuss what the punctuation can mean in terms of more important and less important parts of the message. For example, identifying a pair of parentheses means that for the time being effort should be spent on what is outside the parentheses.
3. Have the students underline connecting expressions at the beginning of or inside the sentence (especially in the neighborhood of internal punctuation). Check to see if they understand what these

connecting expressions mean and what sort of logical organization for the message they set up, such as contrast or causality.

4. Have the students circle (in another color) all the fully conjugated verbs and their auxiliary verbs, if relevant. Often at this point you will see that, among other errors, the students have mistaken gerunds, participials, and modifiers for grammatical verb phrases. In addition, they may be unsure if a preposition is part of an idiomatic verb phrase.

5. Spend some time pointing out why certain words with verblike endings are not fully conjugated. Have them focus on the neighbors of the word to determine why the words do not function as grammatical verbs.

6. After the fully conjugated verbs have been isolated, check to see if the students know their tense and meaning. Then count, with the students, the total number of basic clauses that make up the message.

7. Have the students locate the grammatical subject phrases and discuss issues of difficulty when these subject phrases are distant from the conjugated verb phrase, when they are in nontypical locations, or when they are especially long subject phrases. Help them analyze and decode the meaning of the subject phrases and link every conjugated verb phrase with some subject phrase.

8. Have the students locate all other noun phrases and gerund phrases and help students

- analyze and understand them
- identify which of these word groups is a direct object phrase for a grammatical verb phrase or a prepositional phrase
- find the referents inside or outside the target sentence for all types of pronouns
- supply the implied but missing words in any elliptical structures
- find other lexical links outside the sentence that elements inside the sentence point to (e.g., the words "an additional point" require the reader to go back and find in the previous text at least one previously stated point and connect it with the point in the target sentence)

9. Check to see if the students can link every adjectival phrase to its noun phrase and every adverbial word or phrase to the verb phrase, adjective phrase, or clausal segment it modifies.
10. Help the students with any part of the sentence still not accounted for by the previous steps.
11. Have the students talk through their expanded comprehension of a left-to-right reading of the entire sentence.
12. Give this step-by-step procedure to students written out on a personal card or handout that they can refer to whenever necessary in their reading activities.

Caveats and Options

1. This procedure can be taught ad hoc, should it become apparent that students are struggling with long, difficult sentences, and it can be used as a culminating exercise after a series of individual decoding skills have been overtly taught.
2. It can also be adapted to suit the reading level of the student and the syntactic complexity of the materials the student typically reads. The grammatical terminology used above is mainly for the teacher's benefit in understanding this activity. In teaching the activity, these terms ought to be adjusted to suit the students' knowledge of grammar and grammatical terminology.

Contributor

Sally Jacoby has taught courses in and developed materials for ESL/EFL reading at all levels since 1976.

News Mix

Levels
Intermediate

Aims
Practice reading for
connections between
ideas

Class Time
30 minutes

Preparation Time
30 minutes

Resources
Short newspaper stories

It is important to be able to recognize the meaning-based patterns of organization that link the different sections of a text because such recognition facilitates overall comprehension.

Procedure

1. Choose six news stories each containing three paragraphs.
2. Take the first paragraph of each story, label them 1 through 6 on a worksheet, and photocopy a class set.
3. Cut up the other 2 paragraphs of each text, then mix the 12 paragraphs and arrange them on a worksheet. Photocopy a class set.
4. Ask students to read the first sentence of each story and locate the other two sections of the story, labeling the sections, for example, 1a, 1b, 1c, 2a, 2b, 2c....

Caveats and Options

Use fewer articles, but with more paragraphs.

Contributor

Dino Mahoney is Senior Lecturer at the City Polytechnic of Hong Kong, where, among other things, he is involved with language proficiency course design.

A Memory Game

Levels
Any

Aims
Make students aware of the value of their own knowledge and experience in understanding new information
Demonstrate that information is easier to understand and remember when it is organized

Class Time
15 minutes the first day, 30 minutes the second day

Preparation Time
1 hour +

Resources
Three pictures drawn and colored on newsprint
Three word lists, each written on a piece of newsprint

In this activity, students discover that their own knowledge and experience can assist them in understanding new information and that well-organized information is easier to understand and remember than poorly organized information.

Procedure

1. Tell students they are going to play a memory game: They will see three pictures made with the same pieces, but the pieces will be arranged differently in each picture. They will have 20 seconds to look at each picture and then draw it on their own paper from memory (see Appendix below).
2. Display Picture A, allow students 20 seconds to look at it, take it down, and give them several minutes to draw. Do the same with Picture B, then C.
3. Display all three pictures again, and have students "correct" their own, preferably in a different color. Their homework is to write in a couple of sentences (on the same paper) which picture was easiest to remember, which was most difficult, and why.
4. In the next class, do the word lists in a similar way. Tell students they will have 20 seconds to study each list of words, and then write as many as they can remember.
5. Display List 1, allow students 20 seconds to study it, take it down, and give them several minutes to write as many of the words as they can (on the same piece of paper as their pictures). Repeat with Lists 2 and 3. Before putting up List 3, tell them there is a secret in List 3. If they can find the secret, they can remember the words better.
6. In small groups, have students compare their lists. (After they have worked on this, put the lists up again.) They should then talk about

which pictures and which lists were easiest and hardest to remember and why.

7. Ask different groups for their conclusions and discuss briefly as a class ideas such as:

- Familiar subject matter is easier to read than unfamiliar so reading about familiar topics is a good way for foreign language readers to improve their reading fluency and confidence.
- Readers should actively think about what they read in the light of their own knowledge and experience.
- Looking for the pattern of organization in a reading helps us both understand it and remember the content better.

Caveats and Options

1. If your students are unfamiliar with jack-o-lanterns, you need to use a different image. Choose something they will recognize immediately, make a simple line drawing for Picture C, jumble the same pieces up for Picture A, and arrange them in some organized way (but a way that is not a familiar image) for Picture B.
2. You may want to adjust the viewing time to suit your students. It should be short enough that they can't quite complete most of the tasks, especially Picture A and List 1.
3. Students generally come up with the right observations (e.g., that being familiar with something such as known words or the pumpkin makes it easier to remember and that remembering well-organized things (Picture B, List 2) is easier than trying to remember unorganized things.

Appendix: Sample Drawings and Word Lists

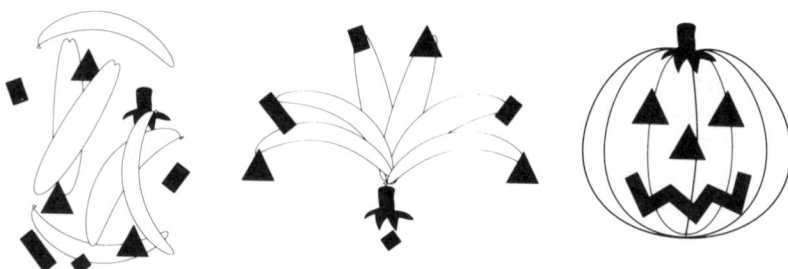

Word List Samples

1	2	3
subway	building	suitcase
tape	window	magazines
mirage	door	library
war	floor	horse
dessert	sports	books
aberration	golf	animals
scientist	soccer	travel
hope	basketball	passport
clock	garden	desks
eternity	flowers	camera
spoon	trees	elephant
heat	grass	dog

Contributor

Nancy Whisler Mutoh received an MA in ESL from the University of Hawaii. She is a permanent faculty member at the Nagoya University of Foreign Studies, Nagoya, Japan.

◆ Scanning
Do-It-Yourself Jigsaw Materials

Levels
Low intermediate +

Aims
Practice scanning
authentic texts

Class Time
20 minutes

Preparation Time
30 minutes

Resources
Three or four
newspaper or magazine
articles on the same
topic

Caveats and Options

Contributor

You can take advantage of media fads to bring articles on high-interest topics into class and to point out to students how useful it is to know something about the topic of a text before reading it.

Procedure

1. Locate suitable articles. Biographies of the latest stars from an assortment of magazines work well. These profiles often appear when a celebrity is publicizing a new movie or television show. Choose 10 facts that are included in at least one of the articles (e.g., hometown, likes, and dislikes). It is best for a gap to exist, that is, one student in a small group should know information the others do not.
2. Circle the paragraphs where the facts appear. Include some distracters.
3. Give an equal number of paragraphs to each member of a pair or group. Also give the group a list of the facts to look for.
4. Ask students to work together to compile the information.

1. The activity can be timed to add an element of competition. The first group to find all the information wins.
2. Tapes of radio or television shows featuring interviews with the stars can be used as authentic listening comprehension material if you want to create an integrated skills exercise.

Steven Brown is on the staff of the University of Pittsburgh English Language Institute in Pennsylvania. He is a co-author of the English Firsthand *and* English Firsthand Beginners' Course *text series.*

Scanning Races

When readers can scan efficiently, they can locate specific information quickly and confidently—an indispensable skill for all learners when they need access to the discrete details in sources ranging from newspapers to chemistry textbooks to telephone books.

Procedure

1. Locate the information you want the students to find and circle it on your copy. Make a note of information stated in more than one place.
2. Divide the class into two teams. Give the word or information that they are to find. When the person who locates the information first signals readiness, verify the answer. If it is incorrect, go to the other team to see if they have found it. If they are still looking, then wait for someone from either team to volunteer.
4. When the information has been correctly located, proceed with another item.

Caveats and Options

1. Students can become rather excited during this activity, so I recommend using it at the end of class. Different types of information may be used, such as names of people or places, or quotes. The level of difficulty can be varied by altering the size of the area the information may be found. For example, at the start of a course on newspapers, you might ask the students to look for place names on the front page. At the end of the term, they could be looking through the entire paper for weather information or sports scores without cues from you as to where to look.
2. Keep score and award points for each correct answer.
3. Add items that cannot be found as distracters.

4. Call the game "Geography Races," and use the same procedure to locate places on maps.

Contributor

Caroline Crolley is a candidate for an MA in ESL at the University of Hawaii, where she also teaches.

Scanning Newspapers and Magazines

Levels
High beginning +

Aims
Practice scanning
newspaper or magazine
articles

Class Time
30 minutes

Preparation Time
45 minutes

Resources
Short, unabridged
newspaper or magazine
article

Students have many constraints on their time. If we want them to take advantage of the information in newspapers—news about their countries, news about our communities—we need to help them find specific information in them quickly.

Procedure

1. Locate a suitable newspaper article with specific details.
2. Write two sets of questions based on the article. If the students are beginning readers, put the questions in the order in which they will be found in the article. If students are intermediate or advanced readers, mix the questions. Write the answers under the questions.
3. Label one set of questions *A* and the other set *B*. At the right of each question leave a space marked *Time* (where the students can record the amount of time it took their partner to find the answer).
4. Put the students in pairs. Give one student a copy of the newspaper article and the other student one set of questions and answers (*A* or *B*). Instruct the students to start with the first question and let them know when to begin.
5. One student reads the questions and the other listens, reads, and gives the answer. If the student is not correct, the partner says that the student should try again. If the answer is correct, both should raise their hands.
6. When you see them raising their hands, write on the blackboard the amount of time that has elapsed since you told them to begin looking for the answer to the question. The student with the questions and answers looks at the blackboard for the time and then writes it down in the space provided.

7. Wait for the whole class to finish before starting the second question. Have the students changed roles half way through.
8. At the end of the reading, the pair with the least time noted is the winner.

Contributor

Patricia Galien is Assistant Professor in the English Language Program, Obirin University, Tokyo, Japan. She has been in Japan for many years.

Read and Run

Levels
Beginning–intermediate

Aims
Practice scanning for
information
Exercise learners'
memories

Class Time
15–20 minutes

Preparation Time
5 minutes

Resources
A reading text with
comprehension
questions
Enlarged copies of the
text

Learners need to know what they are reading for. By looking at questions before they read, they are better able to understand the text and scan for the necessary information.

Procedure

1. Divide the reading in half. Post the enlarged copies of first half on the front wall and the second half on the back wall.
2. Divide the class into pairs, *A* and *B*. Divide the questions and assign half to the *As* and half to *Bs* (e.g., "*As*, you must answer questions 1 through 5. The answer in this part of the reading." [point to the copies on the front wall] *Bs*, you answer 6 through 10. The answers are in that part." [point to the copies on the back wall]).
3. When you tell them to start, all *As* ask the first question to their partners. The partners run to the texts posted on the front wall and scan for the answer. When they find the answer, they run back to *A* and tell the answer. *A* writes it, then asks the next question. Half-way through the activity, they change roles; *B* asks while *A* reads and runs.

Caveats and Options

This activity works best with literal comprehension questions. Because learners engage in physical activity, it is especially useful for involving unmotivated students or at times of the year when many learners have difficulty concentrating because of weather, upcoming events, or other distractions.

Contributor

Marc Helgesen teaches at Miyagi Gakuin, Sendai, Japan. He is the co-author of several ESL texts, including English Firsthand, New English Firsthand, *and* New English Firsthand Plus.

True/False?

Levels
Any

Aims
Give readers a purpose
for reading

Class Time
15–30 minutes

Preparation Time
15–20 minutes

Resources
Passages from students'
reading text or from
other sources

Readers need to develop a wide range of reading skills. Skimming and scanning skills are used naturally in this activity as students reread to find answers.

Procedure

1. Make up True/False questions for the passage you have selected. Include questions that cannot be answered because the information is not in the passage.
2. Ask the students to read the selected passage (see Appendix below).
3. Put the students into pairs and ask them to answer the True/False questions. They can only have one answer for each question.
4. When the students have completed the exercise, discuss the answers as a class. Encourage students to use skimming and scanning skills to respond to inconsistencies among their answers.

Appendix: Sample Passage and Questions

Once there was an old, old man who lived by himself in a small hut in a quiet forest. The old man didn't always live by himself. When he was younger, he lived in a large city where there were many, many different kinds of people.
1. The old man lived in a small house in the woods. (T)
2. The old man moved to the forest when he was old.(?)
3. The city was near the forest.(?)
4. There was only one kind of person in the city. (F)

Contributor

Katharine Isbell is the Program Developer and an instructor for the Asahi Chemical Industry Co. employee English program in Nobeoka, Japan. Previously, she was a teacher trainer in Thailand and Indonesia.

Catalogue Jigsaw

Levels
Intermediate +

Aims
Practice reading for
specific information in
U.S. college and
university catalogue

Class Time
30 minutes

Preparation Time
15 minutes

Resources
One catalogue each
from five different
colleges or universities

Students need to practice scanning so that they can build their reading strategies. They need to become familiar with college and university catalogues so that they know how to locate information in them.

Procedure

1. Give students questions that they are going to answer by examining college or university catalogues. Questions might include items such as: *How many students attend the school? Does the college/university offer BA or BS degrees in nursing, engineering, and business administration? How large is the campus? Approximately how many buildings are there?*
2. Divide the class into five groups and give each group one college or university catalogue.
3. Have group members take turns looking in the group's catalogue to search for information to answer the questions.
4. Ask group members to share information and take notes so that each of them can answer all of the questions about their catalogue.
5. When all students the answers to the questions, they should number off in their groups. Then all of the "ones" form a new group, the "twos" form a new group, and so forth. These new groups should consist of one member from each of the previous groups.
6. In the new groups, students take turns telling the other group members information about the college or university that they researched in their previous group.

Caveats and Options

1. Instead of using college or university catalogues, locate recruitment brochures on five colleges and universities. Repeat the given steps while substituting recruitment materials.

2. After students have already looked at one set of college or university catalogues, repeat the procedure with another set of catalogues. This time the class could brainstorm questions they would like to research in the new set of catalogues.
3. This task is particularly effective when it is part of a unit on higher education in the United States.

References and Further Reading

Lipp, E., & Davis, D. (1992). *Building effective language learning strategies through academic units.* Paper given at the 26th Annual TESOL Convention, Vancouver, Canada.

Contributors

Ellen Lipp teaches linguistics at California State University at Fresno and directs its ESL program. Debbie Davis is Assistant Director of the ESL program at CSU and also an instructor.

Where Shall We Go?

Levels
Intermediate

Aims
Practice scanning for information in authentic texts related to holidays and travel

Class Time
20 minutes

Preparation Time
1 hour

Resources
Colorful travel brochures offering package holidays

Students acquire confidence and refine their scanning skills when they look for information that interests them in authentic texts. Travel brochures give everyone a chance to indulge a fantasy about a dream holiday.

Procedure

1. Collect three class sets of travel brochures. These are usually readily available from travel agencies.
2. Prepare a set of four different role cards, with enough sets for the class. Each role card should have a brief character profile of members of a family, or a group of friends, for example. The card should also have a short list of preferences for each character for a certain kind of holiday, including, for example, country, state, location, type of residence, facilities, and cost. There should be some variation in preference among the different group members.
3. Put students into groups of four and distribute a set of the role cards to each group, assigning a role card to each student in the group.
4. Ask students to scan the travel brochures for the information their character would need and then to role play a holiday planning situation. Their task is to arrive at a decision about where to go on holiday.

Contributor

Dino Mahoney is Senior Lecturer at the City Polytechnic of Hong Kong, where, among other things, he is involved with language proficiency course design.

Finding the Ad

Levels
Intermediate +

Aims
Practice scanning skills
in an authentic context

Class Time
20–30 minutes

Preparation Time
30 minutes–1 hour

Resources
Classified newspaper
ads or bulletin boards
with a wide variety of
ads, such as those on a
university campus

Reading a classified section of a newspaper or a movie listing helps students practice scanning for specific information that may be useful to them outside the classroom. This activity asks them to peruse the classifieds on a public ad board for a good deal on a car or apartment.

1980 Honda Prelude in good condition, needs body work. Yours for the right price.

1978 Toyota blue 4-door. 35,000 miles, manual, air conditioning, Looks + runs excellent. $4,000 or best offer. Call 104-555-4321.

1980 VW. Almost new, mint condition.

Procedure

1. Scan the ad board first to see what selection and spectrum of advertisements are available.
2. Create lists of requirements of different objects to purchase or apartments to rent (e.g., *I only have $1,000 but live far from campus and need to commute to school; if I buy a car, I don't want a sports car; I can't drive standard; the car must be newer than 1985...*). Your requirements do not need to correspond to specific ads, but should be specific enough that students will be able to make judgments based on them.
3. Group the students, distributing one list of requirements to each group.
4. Send the groups out to ad boards on campus, giving them a time limit or incentive to be the first group to return.
5. When all groups have returned, have each group share their results.

Caveats and Options

Prepare an exercise asking students to find information in the different parts of a textbook (e.g., chapters, index, table of contents).

Contributor

Tee Swan has taught in China and at the University of Hawaii.

Seeking and Finding

Levels
Young learners who already know the alphabet and some basic phonics

Aims
Demonstrate that the words in a textbook are recognizable and accessible

Class Time
5–10 minutes

Preparation Time
No set time

Resources
A dialogue presented as a cartoon

Scanning, finding and recognizing chunks of text, and oral reading are the skills practiced in this activity. The cartoon format and the possibility of some nonthreatening competition make it an enjoyable alternative to traditional methods of presenting dialogues.

Procedure

1. Read through (or play a tape of) a dialogue that is presented as a cartoon, with numbered squares for each exchange (see Appendix below).
2. Read any portion at random and ask students to show where it is (by either giving the number or pointing to it). Continue this for some time, until students have a good grasp of the entire text.
3. Ask students to read the dialogue out loud themselves.

Caveats and Options

1. When certain words appear repeatedly, you can read through the dialogue once, then ask students to find how many times a word occurs. Students locate various words in this way until they are ready to read the passage themselves.
2. A text like *American English Today* (Howe, 1987) is suitable because it utilizes a cartoon format with numbered squares, or uses numbered sentences. *American English Today* (particularly Book 3) sometimes presents on one part of a page a long list of numbered or lettered questions or phrases that students are supposed to match with pictures on another part of the page. Instead of going through such a list mechanically, you can easily make the activity into a race to match pictures and text. Working either individually or in teams,

students race to write the number of the right question or phrase over the right picture. The first student or team to finish all of them correctly wins.

References and Further Reading

Howe, D. H. (1987). *American English today.* New York: Oxford University Press.

Contributor

Matthew Taylor has taught in Nagoya, Japan for many years and has recently obtained an MA TESOL degree from Columbia University Teachers College, Tokyo.

10 **A puzzle.**

Appendix: Sample Dialogue and Questions

Ask or answer the questions:

1. Who's cooking?
2. Who's drinking?
3. Who's swimming?
4. Who's running?
5. Who's sleeping?
6. Who's eating?
7. Who's crying?
8. Who's riding a bicycle?
9. Who's flying an airplane?
10. Who's hopping?
11. Who's painting?
12. Who's jumping?
13. Who's singing?
14. Who's cutting?
15. Who's walking?
16. Who's driving a car?

Mary   Mike   Ann   Teresa   Sarah   Susan

Helen   Peter   John   Mabel   David   Mark

Sam

From Howe, D. H. (1987). *American English today.* (Book 2). New York: Oxford University Press. Page 2 used with permission of Oxford University Press.

Look and say.

From Howe, D. H. (1987). *American English today.* (Book 3). New York: Oxford University Press. Page 10 used with permission of Oxford University Press.

Match the Well-Known Story

Levels
Any

Aims
Practice skimming and scanning

Class Time
15–40 minutes

Preparation Time
20–30 minutes

Resources
Well-known stories from either graded readers or original books

Effective readers can identify paragraphs or passages quickly by glancing at the whole text and by searching for key words, rather than looking at each word in order. In this activity, pictures remind the reader of a well-known story, making it easier to scan for particular words or phrases.

Procedure

1. Choose five to eight well-known stories such as *Peter Pan*, *Wizard of Oz*, *Daddy Long-Legs*, *The Little Prince*, or others.
2. Choose one or two short paragraphs from each story. The section must include some hints about the story, such as the character's name, a location, or a famous line. Copy the pages, cut and paste the paragraphs in random order, and number them. Include a blank next to the paragraphs for the titles of the stories.
3. Find a picture or an illustration from each book that describes the story well. Copy, cut, and paste the pictures randomly on a different piece of paper. On the same paper, cut and paste a few unrelated pictures from other well-known stories and mix them in. Number the pictures.
4. Distribute the two kinds of handouts (one with paragraphs and one with pictures) to the students. Ask them to match the paragraphs and pictures as quickly as possible. Students also have to write their guess of the titles of the books.
5. After students have finished matching, ask them to circle the words or phrases that became hints for identifying the stories.
6. Have students compare their circled phrases with those of other students.
7. This activity can be done in a pleasant but competitive atmosphere. It might be a good practice to have to search for the information in

a short time. (In my class, I allow 15 minutes for my best students.) However, if you or the students do not like competition, conduct the activity in a more relaxed way.

Contributor

Junko Yamanaka is Academic Director of Trident School of Languages, Nagoya, Japan.

Creating an Individualized Scanning Center

Levels
Low intermediate +

Aims
Practice scanning
authentic materials
Offer exposure to a
variety of printing sizes,
styles, and layouts

Class Time
5–10 minutes

Preparation Time
10 minutes per card

Resources
Realia such as
schedules, maps, labels,
tables of contents,
handwritten recipes, ads
Cutting knife, rule,
spray glue, light
cardboard

S tudents improve their reading skills by scanning useful, everyday sources of information. This activity offers students a chance to practice their scanning skills individually.

Procedure

1. Make copies of the realia, enlarging only if necessary. If the text is too long, break it up in a logical way (e.g., Museum Hours, List of Exhibitions). Add a title if the source is not obvious.
2. Type three or four questions that a native speaker would be able to answer by scanning the text (e.g., *What is the admission fee?*) Arrange questions in order of increasing difficulty. Type answers also.
3. Trim reading materials; use spray glue to paste reading materials and questions on the front of each card; paste answers on the back.
4. In class, allow students to choose their own cards. There should be a time limit (e.g., 5 minutes for at least two cards) to keep students scanning as quickly as possible. Students should keep a record of their progress, whether in terms of time, number of cards scanned, or number of correct answers.

Caveats and Options

1. Try to have half again as many cards as you have students, or use cards for small-group work in conjunction with other activities.
2. Keep adding to your scanning materials file and make more cards later when you have time.

Contributor

Suzanne Yonesaka is Associate Professor at Hokkaigakuen University in Sapporo, Japan.

◆ Skimming
Find My Answer

Levels
Intermediate +

Aims
Practice skimming and
scanning
Increase vocabulary and
reading speed

Class Time
50 minutes

Preparation Time
None

Resources
Newspapers

It is important for students to know that they don't have to read every word to find information they need. This activity, which exercises students' developing skimming and scanning skills, uses newspapers—a natural source of discrete information to scan for and of global stories to skim.

Procedure

1. Give each student one page from a newspaper, with two articles highlighted.
2. Ask the students to read their two articles and write a question based on one of them at the top of the page without indicating which article their question comes from.
3. After the students have finished, have them move around the class and try to answer four of their classmates' questions. They must state the name of the article as well as the answer.
4. After everyone has circulated, have students return to their seats. Ask who found the answer to any particular student's question. Have said student verify the answer. Continue this until the class has checked all the answers.
5. Ask the students to choose two of the most interesting articles for reading practice in the next class.

Contributor

Kelley M. Fast is an ESL instructor, Department of Applied Language Studies, Brock University, Ontario, Canada.

Compare the Two

Levels
Intermediate +

Aims
Read with a purpose
and for pleasure
Recognize social and
cultural differences
between texts in two
languages

Class Time
60–90 minutes

Preparation Time
15 minutes

Resources
One page of a well-
known novel or
nonfiction text written
in the students' native
language and its
published English
translation

If they have a bilingual text, students can read with a real purpose and want to read the English text over and over again. This activity defies the conventional wisdom that translations hinders instruction and learning.

Procedure

1. If you are fluent in the L1 of your students, copy a page of a well-known novel or nonfiction text. Then find the English equivalent of that page from the translated book and copy it.
2. If you are a native speaker of English, copy a page of an English translation of a well-known piece written in the students' native language. Find the equivalent page of the original and copy it.
3. Distribute the two kinds of copies (one in English and one in the students' native language).
4. Tell the students to skim both copies. They can choose the order (L1 first, then English, or vice versa).
5. Distribute blank sheets of paper, telling the students to read carefully and write on the paper the parts (e.g., phrases, sentences) where the translation could not fully express the nuance of the original work and where the translation is so good that it expresses the nuance even better than the original.
6. Require students to give reasons for their opinions.

Caveats and Options

I've used this activity successfully several times with students of different levels, but it works best with students of higher levels. Because it allows the students to perceive English as a real language, they *do* read the passages more carefully.

Contributor

Junko Yamanaka is Academic Director of Trident School of Languages, Nagoya, Japan.

◆ Academic Reading Student-Led Reading Groups

Levels
Intermediate +

Aims
Expand the kinds of reading students do outside of class
Provide a setting in which students can share responses to what they've read

Class Time
25–30 minutes

Preparation Time
No set time

Resources
Magazines or short stories

Students need to get used to reading large amounts of material in preparation for later college assignments. They also need to make choices about what they read and then have the opportunity to discuss their views on what they've read with others.

Procedure

1. Ask students for their college or intended majors and other areas of interest. Use this information to group them in "interest groups" of four people. Groups are flexible; students can change them if they wish. Sample groups might include one with a business focus, one with an engineering focus, one with a history focus.
2. Each week, ask groups to designate one member (different each week) as responsible for finding a short story or magazine article. This person is to bring enough copies of the text to class for every other person in the group.
3. After spending the week reading the text outside of class, groups should be ready to discuss in class the article or short story they have read. Discussion is open-ended, depending on what they are interested in talking about. Some possibilities: main idea, vocabulary, their reactions.
4. During the last 5 minutes, have a member of each group quickly fill out the *Reading Group Report* (see Appendix below), with the input of the rest of the group. Collect the reports and monitor the activity.
5. Repeat the process.

Appendix: Reading Group Report

Group members _____   Week No. _____

_____

_____

Assignment: Short story   Magazine article   Other _____

Title _____

Author and/or Magazine _____

Total Number of Pages _____

Number of Pages Completed _____

Difficult?   No   Average   Yes
Interesting?   No   Average   Yes

How much time spent reading? Not much   Average   A lot
Do you recommend this reading? Yes   No

Why or why not? _____

In-class discussion	Vocabulary	Meaning	Content
	Ideas	Reaction	Other _____
Success of activity	Low	Average	High
Comments			

Contributor

Patricia Brenner, teacher trainer, author, consultant, and ESL instructor at the University of Washington, has taught in Iran, Germany, Greece, and the United States. She taught in Ankara, Turkey, as a Fulbright recipient.

Reading and Responding: Using Journals

Levels
Any

Aims
Promote second
language development
Contribute to students'
overall education

Class Time
No set time

Preparation Time
No set time

Resources
Any reading materials
Journals
Guidelines

Second and foreign language reading activities can be much more than language teaching tools. They can, additionally, motivate student interest in foreign language and culture and trigger explorations into self that contribute to intellectual and personal growth. Indeed, I believe that the most successful classroom reading activities benefit students in at least these two ways: by promoting second language development and by contributing to students' overall education. Students who read with comprehension and fluency, in a first or a second language, but who do not reflect on what they read in ways that are personally meaningful, are neglecting one of the most powerful and long-lasting benefits of reading. Reading, in other words, can involve more than comprehension. It may also include responding—through thought, talk, and writing—in ways that promote educational and intellectual growth.

I'd like to discuss just one of those ways of responding—writing—with the understanding that thinking and talk are necessarily part of the total process when we design reading activities: Students should think, talk, and write about what they read, before, during, and after. But writing has the special capacity to help students push their thinking deeply and to foster meaningful learning (Langer & Applebee, 1987). It does this in part by providing them with time for reflection as well as something to reflect on. It also provides a language and thought outlet—a voice, as it were—for the silent student.

Procedure

1. Select readings that are built around an issue that can provoke interest, even if the specifics of the topic do not suit all students equally. Consider why you are asking students to read something. One valu-

able purpose consists of reading to learn something about oneself and one's culture. If this is one of our purposes, we will not so easily fall back into comfortable habits of asking students to read in order to remember irrelevant information from a text just to show us that they can do reading skills exercises and activities. If the purpose is to help students engage with text as a way to learn about themselves, the problem of selecting texts becomes easier. We look for texts that spark issues that relate to our particular group of students.

2. Prepare journal guidelines. Once students have begun to think about an issue in ways that are relevant to their own lives, they are ready to read and respond to the reading. Responding by writing a journal requires some guidance from teachers if students have not written journals before. Students need to understand, for example, that a reading response journal is not a retelling of what the text was about. In my journal requirements, I tell students they don't even need to summarize or take notes unless they want to for their own purposes. This is because I want them to liberate themselves from the long-standing tradition, in Japan at least, of never having to go beyond learning what's in the text.

   Journal writing guidelines, then, conveyed in writing, in discussion and through examples of the teacher's own journal or the journals of previous students, should be prepared carefully and reinforced as students write their first journals. A set of good handouts is helpful, one general and one specific to particular readings.

3. Prepare general guidelines. General guidelines should describe the overall purpose of journal writing that is done in response to reading (or to film, discussion, and lecture, for that matter) and set out the parameters of the task for the particular class. For example, I always write in my guidelines what the minimum length (in words) should be, how often journals have to be turned in, and what my criteria are for evaluating them because individual journals do not get a grade. I also remind them to keep all journals in a folder so that they can periodically go back over them and monitor change in their language and thinking.

   I prepare students not to receive much feedback on language, assuring them that this will take place elsewhere in the course, and try to convey a sense of what the journal writing literature says about the value of continuous extensive writing (hence the length requirement) for language development and for depth of thinking. I then describe more specifically what students should do in their journals. Here is an excerpt from the general guidelines for the advanced students (a simpler version is prepared for the lower levels):

What should you do in your journals? You should respond to issues and ideas from your readings. Please don't tell what the readings are about, except to make it clear which reading and which idea from it you are talking about. Respond to ideas in the readings that strike you as interesting, important, personally relevant, and so on. Here are some things you can do in your journals:

- Write about an event, issue, or idea in the reading that strikes you as important, interesting, or surprising. Tell why it is so, if possible.
- Relate what you read to something in your own life, experience, or culture.
- Explore an issue by asking questions about it in writing and trying out several different answers or solutions. It's OK to end with questions! Getting educated, after all, is partly a matter of learning how to ask better and better questions.
- Tell why you think that aspects of a reading were good or bad. Explain why if possible.
- Evaluate an issue in your own life or culture that is similar to an issue in a reading.
- Express opinions, doubts, confusions, and convictions that come to your mind as you think about what you have read. Watch and write about how these change over time.

These general journal guidelines may be all that is needed, depending on the experience of students with journal writing and on the kinds of readings that a class is doing. In some cases, such as with students who have not written journals before or in the case of particularly difficult readings, it may be useful to prepare specific journal writing guidelines.

4. Prepare specific guidelines. Specific written guidelines can help orient students to the task of journal writing and can allow teachers to guide students through the issues in texts that are too difficult for them to read on their own without feeling defeated. In early journal guidelines, for my advanced students, I prepared two kinds of questions that were designed to achieve both these purposes: "questions at the level of information" and "questions at the level of response."

Questions at the level of information help students skip over details and focus on key issues in texts that are especially long or difficult. Long and difficult texts should not necessarily be avoided, in other words, because once out of our classes, this is what students will encounter, especially if they continue using their second language to further their education. Such questions should be clearly marked on handouts as information questions and not response questions. An example from the readings on intelligence with the advanced Japanese students draws students' attention to the issue of how people in different cultures and professions decide who is intelligent and who is not. From a chapter of Gould's *The Mismeasure of Man* are the following journal guide questions at the level of information. Note that the questions themselves are important sources of collected vocabulary that we would expect to appear in students' journals later and that they encapsulate some of the main ideas from the readings:

- Gould tells us that Louis Agassi had no data to support his theory about the inferiority of Blacks. What kinds of data ("empirical evidence") did Samuel George Morton have? How did he measure cranial capacity?
- Morton was considered an excellent scientist in the mid 1800s because his methods of analyzing his data were considered to be very objective and very precise (and therefore very fair and unbiased). However, Gould says that Morton used his data to prove a view that he already held about the intelligence of different races. Gould was thus skeptical about Morton's findings. What did he do?
- What did Gould discover about Morton's analysis? (How did Morton manage to "fudge" his data?)

Questions at the level of response also emerge out of the readings, but ask students to engage with an issue, not with textual facts, in personally meaningful ways and at some depth. From the same reading in *The Mismeasure of Man*, I devised the following response-level questions:

- Imagine that you are a scientist in 1850. Somebody told you about the work of Samuel George Morton and what he was trying to prove. You do not like the fact that he had already decided which races were superior to others, so you decide to analyze the same 600 skulls that he did, but without a preconceived idea, to the extent possible. How would you try to measure these skulls so that your measurements were not biased?
- In general, what are the Japanese people's opinions about scientists? Do they tend to believe what scientists say? To be skeptical of what they say? What is your own opinion?

In short, these two kinds of questions help students distinguish between two very different ways of interacting with text. Both are important, but the personal responses will stimulate interest and depth of thinking in ways that information questions do not. When the specific information fades from memory, the issue will still be there if students have made it their own.

5. Respond to journals. Journals to which teachers do not respond may nevertheless be valuable in the sense that students have read, thought, written at length, and dealt with language and with issues. But a personal response from a teacher, no matter how minimal, sets up a communication that students find more rewarding than many other kinds of less personal interactions in a language class. Yet it is the case that most of us have so little time that the thought of reading and responding to 50 or 100 journals every week or two boggles the mind. There are shortcuts as well as compromises and compensations.

The first shortcut/compromise involves great will power on the part of teachers to resist marking language errors. The second involves the will power to resist commenting on every idea or even every paper. For example, I often just put a check or line next to a passage that I find particularly interesting so that students know I have attended to it. The third involves developing the skill to make most comments brief but meaningful for the student (not just *good* in the margin, but *I agree,* or *Why/How?* or *Interesting!*) and occasionally astounding some of them with a lengthy inquiry-type response of your own. Another compromise can be to write your own journal back to the students—one lengthy response to everyone—in which you touch on the issues raised by them in their journals. Another idea, which should be handled delicately because of the personal nature of some of the journals, is peer reading and oral or written response. A compromise on the question of linguistic feedback, which some students may persist in requesting, is to extract passages anonymously from the journals and write them on an overhead to be reviewed later for lexical, grammatical, and stylistic improvements.

But it may be that teachers will find that reading journals is not as tedious as they expected and that it comes to be a central aspect of their interaction with students. I have found that the labor-intensive nature of responding to journals is usually well worth the time. I learn more about the students' language ability, personalities, and interests than I ever could without journals (I have 60–100 students a semester), am able to design subsequent classes that fit their needs and interests, and receive invaluable feedback on class activities. Furthermore, it is exciting to watch a young mind explore an issue never before explored and write more English than he or she has ever before written, much to the writer's amazement and delight. I often find that a lengthy response happens rather effortlessly as I become caught up in an interesting idea.

The ways in which a teacher responds will influence students' subsequent journal efforts, the quality of their thinking, their engagement with subsequent readings, and their personal relationship with teachers. Teachers have the capacity, without making lengthy responses to every student's journal every time, of setting up a regular and meaningful communication with students that will help them understand what it means to respond thoughtfully to a text and why reading and responding can become a language class activity that they can "own."

6. Read and respond. This technique for teaching reading, perhaps unfortunately, cannot easily be set down and standardized in textbook form. To work well, readings, issues, discussion activities, journal requirements, and types of teacher responses must be adapted anew with each new class.

   With some groups, teachers may wish to help students liberate their thinking—lose their fear of making linguistic errors and of exploring heretofore unimagined original thoughts. With other groups, teachers may wish to help students reflect on language, issues, and themselves in more systematic, less free-for-all ways. Moreover, although I have focused on journal writing here, responding to reading can and should take many forms—oral, written, even artistic—with the result that the total picture in a specific classroom is complex, interactive, and unique to that classroom.

Caveats and Options

1. For additional ideas on communicative prereading activities, see Casanave (1986) and Casanave and Williams (1987).
2. A good source book for teachers unfamiliar with journal writing is Fulwiler (1987).
3. I have explored some of these aspects of journal writing in Casanave (1992).

References and Further Reading

Casanave, C. P. (1986). *Strategies for readers: A reading/communication text for students of ESL.* (Books 1 & 2). Englewood Cliffs, NJ: Prentice Hall.

Casanave, C. P. (1992). Educational goals in the foreign language class: The role of content-motivated journal writing. Keio University SFC *Journal of Language and Communication, 1,* 77-97.

Casanave, C. P., & Williams, D. (1987). *The active reader: An introductory reading/communication text for students of ESL.* Englewood Cliffs, NJ: Prentice Hall.

Fulwiler, T. (Ed.). (1987). *The journal book.* Portsmouth, NH: Boynton/Cook.

Gould, S. J. (1981). *The mismeasure of man.* New York: W. W. Norton.

Langer, J. A., & Applebee, A. N. (1987). *How writing shapes thinking: A study of teaching and learning.* Urbana, IL: National Council of Teachers of English.

Contributor

Christine Pearson Casanave is Associate Professor of English at Keio University's Fujisawa campus in Japan. Her interests include second language reading and writing, disciplinary socialization, and teacher education.

The Reading Contract

Levels
Advanced

Aims
Help students
understand the reasons
for reading
Help them determine
appropriate reading
strategies
Help them generalize
what they learn in the
ESL reading class to
their academic courses

Class Time
15–20 minutes

Preparation Time
No set time

Resources
Copies of a reading
contract

Appendix: Sample Reading Contract

Effective readers are aware of various reading strategies and use them appropriately. Students can learn to change strategies depending on the type of text they are reading and their reasons for reading it. This activity assumes that the students are already aware of and understand the reasons for reading and can use a variety of reading strategies. It is an adaptation of an activity proposed by Jeff Popko for an ESL reading course at the English Language Institute, University of Hawaii.

Procedure

1. Prepare copies of a reading contract (see Appendix below).
2. Explain to the students that this course will focus on the reading they do for their other academic courses and that they will make contracts with you to do such reading. Let them know how many contracts they must complete during the course.
3. Distribute copies of the reading contract and review its requirements. Direct students to complete the first part of the form *before* reading an assignment and the second half when they are finished.
4. After students hand in a completed reading contract, check it and make a record.

Name: Date:
Reading Assignment for Course:
Title:
Author:

Part I. Complete this before reading the assignment.

1. What is the reason for doing this reading? (e.g., to get a quick, general idea of the test; to prepare for a test)
2. What reading strategy or strategies do you plan to use? (e.g., rapid reading, skimming, scanning, careful reading)
3. What steps will you take in reading this assignment?
   a.
   b.
   c.
   d.
   e.
4. How long is the reading assignment? (e.g., 12 pages, 220 pages)
5. How long do you plan to spend on this reading? _____ minutes or _____ hours

Part II. Complete this part after completing the reading.

1. What reading strategies did you actually use?
2. Was what you actually did different from what you had planned to do? If yes, explain.
3. How much time did you spend on the reading?
4. Did you leave any steps out? If yes, which ones, and why?

Contributor

Richard R. Day, whose early EFL experiences include the Peace Corps in Ethiopia, is Professor of ESL, University of Hawaii.

Charting Patterns

Levels
Advanced

Aims
Improve students'
ability to read academic
texts
Make students aware of
differences in the
writing of different
disciplines and how to
use that knowledge to
enhance their reading
comprehension

Class Time
45 minutes the first day;
15–30 minutes another
day for follow up

Preparation Time
30 minutes–1 hour

This exercise sharpens students' analytical skills and makes them more conscious of appropriate reading strategies for different types of texts. It also enhances students' knowledge of various discourse patterns that commonly appear in texts from different academic disciplines. The exercise thus provides a bridge between the ESL classroom and the real world of reading academic texts for college classes. Because college texts in the different disciplines use various discourse patterns, readers who understand the organizational, structural, and methodological patterns of the discourse in different disciplines are able to read faster and comprehend better.

Procedure

1. Photocopy the blank grid (see Appendix below) or construct a similar one. Give each student two copies of the grid, one for the in-class exercise and one for the homework assignment.
2. Introduce the exercise by talking briefly about the different types of language, organization, methods, and audience that are assumed by writers in different disciplines.
3. Using a very short article that students can read quickly in class, or one that the class has read for another assignment, discuss briefly two or three of the categories listed on the grid. Then, working with the students, fill in comments in each box on the sample grid. (Using pencil will make additions, corrections, and changes easier.)
4. During the next class, divide the students into teams of four to six members.
5. Give each team copies of one short article. Different teams should get articles from different disciplines. Try to have one from the physical sciences, one from the social sciences, and one from humanities.

Have students take the article home to read and ask them to fill in the grid.

6. In a later class, ask individual teams to compare the entries they made on their grids. After each team has reached agreement, it can tell the rest of the class its findings.

Caveats and Options

1. A copy of the chart can be constructed on the board or on an overhead transparency rather quickly. Students can then fill in their comments for the whole class to see, discuss, and compare.

2. This is a high-level exercise, best for students who are ready to begin college work. It is not, however, an exercise in reading comprehension. Articles which may be too technical for students to understand completely will reveal differences in organization, vocabulary, structure, audience, methodology, and sources. This exercise will help students to become aware of those factors and to be more conscious of the reading strategies they need in order to understand materials in different disciplines.

3. In addition to the readings that students may bring from their own classes, materials readily available in ESL readers and classroom materials, and articles gathered from journals in a library, there are several anthologies of readings across the disciplines that provide a wealth of material. (See References and Further Reading.)

References and Further Reading

Arnaudet, M., & Barrett, M. E. (1984). *Approaches to academic reading and writing*. Englewood Cliffs, NJ: Prentice Hall.

Comley, N., Hamilton, D., Klaus, C., Scholes, R., & Sommers, N. (1984). *Fields of writing: Reading across the disciplines*. New York: St. Martin's.

Hillman, L. H. (1990). *Reading at the university*. Boston: Heinle & Heinle.

Leki, I. (1989). *Academic writing: Techniques and tasks*. New York: St. Martin's.

Appendix: Charting Academic Writing Patterns

Element	Text	Text
Type of article/ text (discipline)		
Audience		
Purpose		
Perspective		
Structure and organization		
Language and vocabulary		
Methods		
Kinds of evidence presented		

Element	Text Taylor, W. + T. Baranowski. (1991). Physical Activity, Cardiovascular Fitness, and Ad in Children. Research Quarterly of Exercise + Sport, 62(2), 157 - 163.	Text
Type of article/ text (discipline)	Research Quarterly of Exercise + Sport Disciplines: health, physical education, health research, medical	
Audience	health professionals + researchers, sports researchers, sports medicine practioners, physical education professionals	
Purpose	report on results of a study conducted by the authors on the relationship bet. physical activity, cardiovascular fitness + adiposity	
Perspective	That of researcher + medical professor trying to identify relationships + variants in a set of conditions	
Structure and organization	abstract; intro + summary of earlier studies; description of methodology; results from the study given in narrative form + tables + charts; possible explanations; future research	
Language and vocabulary	very technical adiposity = fat!! acronyms used throughout; assumes reader knows vocab. of discipline; conventions of scientific research — variables, samples, validity	
Methods	controlled study; interobserver reliability assessed + adjusted for; results analyzed statistically	
Kinds of evidence presented	dozens of research articles cited; results of author's study of 186 children was the main evidence presented.	

Contributor

Mary Lee Field, Associate Professor at Wayne State University, has taught reading and reading methodology in Japan, China, Yugoslavia and the United States.

This Looks Familiar

Levels
Intermediate; English for Science and Technology course

Aims
Introduce the use of reading strategies

Class Time
1–2 hours

Preparation Time
1–2 hours

Resources
Content textbooks or academic journals

When students read a text in the target language that contains content with which they are familiar, they can focus on reading and vocabulary recognition strategies. Problem solving and translation activities can let students know how much they have understood. Although many teachers frown on using translation, if students are training for positions that will require them to paraphrase the content of an article for colleagues in their first language, translation is an authentic activity in terms of what students will eventually be required to do with material they read.

Procedures

1. Locate a chapter from a textbook or journal the technical content of which is directed at nonspecialists. Develop a vocabulary, problem solving, translation/interpretation, and main idea comprehension worksheet (see Appendix below).
2. Quickly introduce a selection of reading strategies (e.g., prediction, previewing, skimming, scanning) and explain their purposes.
3. Instruct the students to read the title and subtitles of the article and to use this information to predict the content. Write their predictions on the board and do not erase them.
4. Pass out a vocabulary worksheet. Explain vocabulary cognates that appear in the passage (e.g., method/*metodo*). Ask students to look for cognates that are listed on the worksheet and also to find the words in the text, trying to define them from context to make sure that they are not "false" cognates. Encourage them to find cognates not on the list.
5. Have students solve problems from the text.
6. Have students translate or paraphrase sentences from the text. Then hold a general class discussion of the information.

7. Direct the students back to their earlier predictions. Have them determine how many of their predictions were correct.

Caveats and Options

1. Repeating the activity with a similar text will help students incorporate information from different sources.
2. The example included here is derived from a course for Reading English for Science and Technology at the Universidad de Guadalajara, Facultad de Ciencias Químicas in Mexico. Consequently, the examples here are in Spanish and relate to the topic of chemistry. However, similar activities could be developed for other scientific and technological fields.
3. The application activities in the lesson are intended to become progressively more task based: Students will read technical texts in order to gain information that allows them to solve problems or explain information to other people.

Appendix: Sample Worksheet

1. Word skills. The following words appear in the article. Before you read the text, try to guess the meaning of the words. They may be cognates with Spanish or they may be defined in the context of the passage. The paragraph number for each word is given before the word.

Paragraph	Line	Word	Cognate
1	22	to adapt	adaptar
3	2	absolute	absoluto
7	2	the balance	el balance
9	2	the length	la longitud
14	2	independent	independiente
15	1	complete	completa

2. Problem solving. Solve the following problems based on the information in the text. Then write your answers below.
   a. How many milliliters are there in 3 fluid ounces?
   b. Convert 1 pound 3 ounces to kilograms.
   c. How many liters are there in 1 measuring cup (8 fluid oz.)?
   d. A gasoline tank has a capacity of 18 gallons. Express this capacity in liters.

3. Interpretation. Read the following sentences that appear in the text. Translate them into Spanish in the space provided. If you do not know the exact Spanish word, paraphrase. Try to give the meaning of each sentence.
   a. The metric system of weights and measures is used in all scientific work.
   b. The metric system is very simple.
   c. Chemistry is a quantitative science, and much of the real meaning of chemistry is lost if the mathematical relationships are omitted in its study.
   d. Mass is proportional to weight.
   e. A particular natural event is called a phenomenon.
4. Main ideas. Look at the text again. Then answer the following questions in Spanish.
   a. The authors state the following equation: "Careful observation + Persistent search for truth + Intelligent thought = Progress." What does the equation mean?
   b. What is the main idea of Paragraph 6?
   c. What is the relationship between "a phenomenon," "a hypothesis," and "a theory"?

Contributor

Thom Hudson is Assistant Professor, Department of ESL, University of Hawaii. He has worked on reading projects in the United States, Egypt, and Mexico.

Reading and Discussing Professional Abstracts

Levels
Intermediate +;
medical specialists

Aims
Help students
understand authentic
texts by asking them to
use information in
abstracts to make
decisions

Class Time
45 minutes

Preparation Time
30 minutes

Resources
Abstracts from
professional literature

Caveats and Options

Contributor

Using authentic materials such as medical abstracts helps students acquire knowledge about their specialties and improve their reading skills in English. This activity asks students to form reasoned, medical opinions based on the content of the abstracts.

Procedure

1. Find appropriate abstracts that match the specialties of your students. For example, for students who are training in pediatrics, use pediatric medical abstracts.
2. Prepare suitable questions, focusing on main ideas and those which will allow students to use their prior knowledge of the topic.
3. Distribute the abstracts and questions and assign as homework.
4. In the next class, help the students see how the text is organized. You can do this by preparing a graphic overview of the text, distributing it, and helping students complete the blank overview.
5. Discuss the completed graphic overview orally. Ask students to apply the information to other situations, to evaluate the information, and to use it to solve problems. Suggest that they base their opinions on their own medical specialities (e.g., an internist might give an opinion on a pediatric case).

This activity can also be used with students studying agriculture. For example, postgraduate agricultural engineers could use agricultural case reports and textbooks instead of abstracts.

Emalia Iragiliati teaches at Malang Teachers College in Indonesia, from which she also received an MA in TEFL. Her teaching and research interests include ESP, EAP, sociolinguistics, and cross-cultural understanding.

CALL Reading and Note-Taking Lessons

Levels
Intermediate +

Aims
Read expository texts
for main and supporting
ideas

Class Time
20–30 minutes

Preparation Time
10–15 minutes,
prepared lesson;
1–2 hours, new lesson

Resources
VAX computer system
Expository texts

A CALL reading lesson is a very simple way for students to read expository texts in small chunks. Key words in the center of the screen serve as reminders to the students of the main ideas of the text. Students are able to work at their own pace, although it is possible to clock or even allow them a certain amount of time to finish.

Procedure

1. Read through the available lessons and decide if they suit the content you are interested in teaching.
2. Log onto VAX computer and enter Courseware Authoring System (CAS). Create a group, assign lessons, and then assign students to the group.
3. Have students log onto VAX, entering name of group and lesson. Students will see the title page, followed by a page with directions. Then the lesson, which is divided into two sessions, begins.

In Session 1, the screen is divided into three sections. The top section consists of the reading passage, presented one paragraph at a time. In order to advance the reading, the student pushes the <NEXT SCREEN> key. The middle section displays key words for each paragraph. The bottom section displays whatever notes the student types. The notes simply scroll and are saved automatically by the computer.

Session 2 has three parts. First, the student reviews notes from Session 1 for as long as necessary. Then the student types everything remembered about the lesson; this is scored based on the number of main and supporting ideas recalled from the original text. Next, the student answers 20 multiple choice questions based on the main and supporting ideas of the lesson.

Finally, the student answers questions regarding how s/he feels about the lesson.

Caveats and Options

1. If available lessons do not suit your purpose, choose a different text. Divide the text into paragraphs of no more than 10 lines so that each paragraph fits on the computer screen.
2. Choose one or two key words per paragraph.
3. Write an outline of the text. Prepare a list of synonyms for all key words in the outline.
4. Write multiple choice items to serve as a quiz for the main and supporting ideas.
5. Results from the tests will tell you if students understood the main concepts or if remedial work is needed. Students' notes will be saved automatically and will give you an idea of what the student deemed important enough in the text to write down. This information will be useful for students who do poorly as well as those who do well on the lessons.

Contributors

Joan Jamieson, Leslie Norfleet, and Nora Berbisada are in the Applied Linguistics program in the English department at Northern Arizona University.

Maximizing Their Investment

Levels
Intermediate +

Aims
Develop reading
comprehension skills
and vocabulary
Increase student
motivation by utilizing
student-selected
material
Introduce students to
university textbooks

Class Time
10–20 minutes initial
explanation; 30–45
minutes class discussion
after project completion

Preparation Time
30 minutes

Resources
Instruction sheets
Textbooks
Journals

Caveats and Options

Student motivation is crucial to learning. If they are allowed to choose authentic texts, their investment in the lesson increases, their general reading skills develop, and they become familiar with the language requirements of an academic discipline.

Procedure

1. Write project instructions (See Appendices below) and make copies for students. Instructions should include:

   - What texts the student may use
   - Where the students can find texts
   - Why the student is analyzing these texts
   - How you will assess the student's work.

   Inside Textbooks: What Every Student Needs to Know (Adams, 1989) offers a comprehensive analysis of textbooks and is a valuable tool for formulating guidelines.
2. Locate university or second-hand bookstores that sell textbooks and give their addresses to students.
3. Distribute and explain project instructions.
4. After the project is completed, have students exchange information about textbooks in group or class discussions.
5. Collect written projects for assessment.

1. Text analysis can be used to

   - supply authentic material for vocabulary lessons
   - supplement student observation of mainstream classes

- furnish material for oral presentations
- provide information gap activities
- supply material for silent sustained reading in the classroom.

2. The project can be designed to provide either a major portion of course work or a limited homework assignment.
3. Although the basic idea of the project will remain the same—student analysis of a student-selected text—the flexibility of the design allows you to customize this project for a specific class or student. Students in intermediate ESL classes as well as in advanced classes in preacademic programs benefit from this project and have produced insightful reports. ESL students entering graduate programs can base their projects on academic journals. The idea can also be adapted for adult education classes.

References and Further Reading

Adams, T. W. (1989). *Inside textbooks: What every student needs to know.* New York: Addison-Wesley.

Appendix A: Instructions for a Major Project in an Intermediate Reading Class

Independent Reading Project

The objective of the independent reading project is to introduce you to a textbook in your academic major. If you are undecided about your major, you may choose a textbook from a freshman or sophomore history, science or English literature course. Choosing and obtaining the book are your responsibility although I will help you if you have difficulty in making your selection. You can borrow a book from a friend, buy a used book, or look in the library. You should spend at least 10 hours reading the text. In addition you will be required to turn in a reading journal. The last two class periods will be devoted to your reading project. The reading project and journal together count as 30% of your grade, so you should begin to look at textbooks now to find one that interests you.

Your reading journal should include:

1. a description of the parts of the book (e.g., table of contents, glossary, . . .) and the type of information found in each part

2. a list of vocabulary words that are important to your academic discipline
3. ideas that the textbook describes as central or fundamental to your field
4. any problems you had in using the textbook
5. how you solved problems yourself (e.g., using graphs or illustrations to understand difficult explanations).

Let me know which book you have chosen by _____. Your journal is due on _____. You may submit your journal for a progress report before turning it in to be graded.

Appendix B: Instructions for a Homework Assignment for a High Intermediate Reading Class

Syllabus Exercise

Read the attached syllabus and answer the following questions:

1. What is the name of the course?
2. How many textbooks are used?
3. How many times per week does the class meet?
4. What is the average amount of reading assigned per week?
5. What is the teacher's policy about making up quizzes and tests?
6. How many absences are allowed?
7. What type of questions are on the final exam?
8. How much material is covered on the final exam?

(Note: Teacher supplies syllabus for this exercise)

Textbook Exercise

1. Go to the textbook section of the bookstore. Then complete Questions 2-4.
2. Look at textbooks for two university courses that you would like to take. For example, if you are interested in business, look for two different courses in the business section. If you plan to major in computer science or health, look for courses in those sections.
3. Write down the name of one textbook that is used in each course you have selected. Skim each textbook: Look at the table of contents, the first page of each chapter, and any illustrations or appendices. Take notes so that you can write a short description of the book.

Include the course name, the title of the textbook, the number of chapters in the book, the average number of pages in a chapter, the type of illustrations, and anything else about the book that impresses you—for instance, the price, the graphics, or how interesting or difficult you think it will be to use.

4. Write a *short* paragraph describing each book. On _____ turn in both paragraphs and the answers to the questions in the syllabus exercise.

Appendix C: Detailed Instructions for a Journal for an Advanced Class

Independent Reading Project—Journal

The journal is due on the last day of class. To organize your journal, create the following six sections:

1. Make a survey of the textbook by skimming through it. What information does the title give the reader? How is the textbook organized? What information is given by the chapter or section headings? How are key vocabulary and important concepts highlighted? What kinds of illustrations and graphs are used?
2. Make a list of key vocabulary and give their definitions as they are used in the text. If other forms of the words are important for you to know, list them also—for instance, if the text uses both the noun and verb forms of a word.
3. List the main ideas that the textbook describes as "fundamental to the field."
4. Identify the problems you had when you read for comprehension and how you overcame the problems. For example, did the illustrations help you understand difficult ideas?
5. If you could redesign this book, would you make any changes? Why or why not?
6. Read one section or chapter of the text carefully and write a summary.

Contributor

Michele Kilgore is an ESL instructor at Georgia State University. She has an MS in Applied Linguistics and is working on her PhD.

Clozeline

Levels
Intermediate +

Aims
Improve academic
reading comprehension
skills by focusing on
main and supporting
points
Introduce note-taking
skills through outlining

Class Time
30 minutes

Preparation Time
20 minutes

Resources
A textbook chapter and
an outline

Students must be able to recognize main and supporting ideas in order to understand a text. In turn, they must develop note-taking and outlining skills so that they can review the text later.

Procedure

1. Locate a suitable chapter and outline in a textbook.
2. Do not make any changes in the first two sections and the last section of the outline.
3. Omit the main points of the next two parts of the outline. Leave all of the supporting points as they appear in these sections of the outline.
4. Omit about half of the supporting points in another part of the outline. Leave the key point as is in this section.
5. Omit all of the supporting points in one or more remaining sections of the outline.
6. In class, distribute copies of the reading passage and the cloze outlines. Have students read over the cloze outline before they read the chapter. Ask students to use the cloze outline to help them focus on the main ideas and the key supporting ideas for each section when reading.
7. Have students complete the cloze outline.
8. Create small groups of students. Each group can discuss their responses to one part of the outline. If the group has time, they can discuss other sections as well.
9. Group representatives can report on the main and supporting ideas of each section of the outline to the entire class.

Caveats and Options

1. If the textbook chapter does not have an outline, write one for the chapter first and then make it into a cloze outline.

2. Instead of working with an outline, prepare a cognitive map of the chapter. Then leave some key or supporting ideas blank in the cognitive map.

3. Instead of using an entire textbook chapter, students could read a much shorter passage that is written in textbook style (with clear headings and subheadings). Students then work with an outline or cognitive map as described above.

4. If students are shown this exercise before they begin to read, it can give them something to focus on while they are reading. Filling in the outline gaps is best done during or after reading a textbook chapter. Some ESL textbooks include excerpts from textbooks or passages written in textbook style.

Contributors

Ellen Lipp teaches linguistics at California State University at Fresno and directs its ESL program. Debbie Davis is Assistant Director of the ESL program at CSU and also an instructor.

Perusing Academic Journal Articles

Levels
Advanced; post-baccalaureate

Aims
Acquaint students with the format of academic journals in specific fields of study
Develop general reading and library skills

Class Time
20–50 minutes

Preparation Time
20–30 minutes

Resources
Academic journal articles

Most graduate students will encounter academic journals and benefit from an opportunity to interact with this type of authentic text. This activity is best used in conjunction with a reading text that lets you do a similar exercise with the class as a whole. This helps the students understand the assignment and allows you to explain the skill and answer any questions. The students can then transfer these skills to the journal article.

Procedure

1. Have students find an article that relates to their specific field of study (usually three to five pages, but I regularly receive longer articles, too).
2. Give the students one or more specific tasks to do for each article (e.g., locate the main idea of each paragraph, cite the important definitions, determine the conclusion, locate all the pronouns, and give their referents). Students can do the task in the class (especially if it is an exercise in which you want to control the tempo, e.g., scanning) or they can do the task for homework.
3. Collect the assignment and check (unfortunately this part is somewhat labor intensive although I have developed a system of randomly checking sections of each student's assignment in order to cut down on correcting time).

Caveats and Options

1. It is important to take students on a tour of the library so that they can find articles on their own specific interests.
2. It is possible to do various exercises with one article, but I prefer to give the students the opportunity to read a variety of articles (in the

course of a 10-week quarter the students usually do seven journal assignments).

3. I usually give the students a class day off in order to find the article and read it. I use this time the first couple of weeks to help those students who are having problems using library resources.

Contributor

Jim Rogers is a lecturer at the Intensive English Language Institute, Utah State University. His interests include reading, the lexicon, and bilingualism.

Assessing Reading Strategies Through Note-Taking

Levels
High intermediate +

Aims
Assess reading comprehension strategies and note-taking skills

Class Time
1–2 hours

Preparation Time
10–15 minutes per student

Resources
Academic reading passage
Quiz
Note-taking assessment
Recall protocol
Strategies checklist

Teachers need an efficient and effective means of assessing students' reading comprehension and note-taking skills early in a course. This sample lesson is based on a passage about Navajo and Pueblo Indians, but the activity lends itself to work with any topic.

Procedure

1. In the first lesson, give students the passage and ask them to read in preparation for a practice reading comprehension quiz in a multiple-choice format. They may use dictionaries (of the type they prefer) and ask for help from you.
2. Tell them to take notes on the passage itself and/or on a separate sheet of paper which you provide. Tell them that they will be allowed to look at their notes, but not the original passage, when taking the comprehension test.
3. While students are working, note down what kind of dictionaries they are using (i.e., English-English or other) and, if possible, note how many times they are using dictionaries. Have students note the time that they finish on the passage sheet.
4. After 20 minutes collect passages and hand out the multiple choice quiz.
5. Collect quizzes and notes.
6. In the next lesson, return notes to students and ask them to recall what they read the previous lesson and to write this on a sheet of paper. Tell them that this summary will not be graded and that spelling and punctuation are not important. Give them about 15 minutes in class to write.
7. Collect recalls and notes.

8. Outside of class, analyze their notes by checking the appropriate boxes and making the calculations indicated on the note-taking assessment (see Appendix B below).
9. Score recalls using the recall protocol (see Appendix C below).
10. Return notes, note-taking assessments, and recall protocols to students. Assist students in noting possible areas of strength and weakness in reading comprehension and study skills and in assessing their individual skill priorities.
11. Use the note-taking strategies assessment and the Strategies Checklist (See Appendix D below) to discuss which note-taking strategies are most and least efficient: Reading comprehension is enhanced by being attentive and accurate, avoiding translation, focusing on main ideas rather than details or unimportant vocabulary, paraphrasing rather than copying, and structuring ideas through diagramming.
12. Assist students in comparing student note-taking strategies with their results on recalls. Recall results generally reflect note-taking strategies with readers who focus on main ideas tending to recall the main ideas and readers who focus on details tending to recall details. However, some rare individuals with excellent visual memories may recall both main ideas and details with few or no notes. These tendencies should be evident in the data you have collected and can assist you and the student in individualizing instruction.
13. Use the information you've gained to help chart class and individual student needs.

Caveats and Options

1. Students can be asked to read and take notes in preparation for tutoring another student rather than for a quiz. The results of the quiz or the tutoring session are not important in themselves, but rather serve as a catalyst for study and note-taking, as a possible source of reflection on anxiety students may feel in knowing that they will be tested on or asked to talk about material, and as a possible basis for discussion on ways to minimize this anxiety so that comprehension is not hindered. Our previous research suggests that for some individuals reading for a test or tutoring may elicit anxiety that can in turn influence note-taking strategies.

2. Adapt our materials for a different class level or setting: The expository prose passage needs to be challenging, but readable for the particular students in your class. For advanced students such a passage might come from an SAT manual, as ours did, from reading texts, or from other sources.
3. The note-taking strategies assessment sheet can be used to analyze the notes for any academic reading passage.
4. Recall analyses can be created for most reading passages following our pattern. For detailed instructions on the creation of recall protocols see Baumann (1988).

Baumann, J. F. (1988). *Reading assessment: An instructional decision-making perspective*. Columbus, OH: Merrill.

References and Further Reading

Appendix A: Multiple Choice Test

Directions: Choose the one best answer to the following questions.
1. The main purpose of the passage is to
   a. describe how Navajos knew when it was too late to plant their crops.
   b. describe how the Navajos knew that the first autumn frost would be in September.
   c. describe two different calendars used by the Navajos and the Pueblos.
   d. describe how the constellation Dilyehe was first seen near summer solstice in the early morning sky to the northeast after having been absent for several months.
   e. describe how the Navajos and Pueblos used calendars to leave archaeological remains of their astronomical observations.
2. Which of the following can be inferred from the passage about the use of the night sky for constructing a calendar?
   a. It is less reliable than the use of the Sun and the Moon for such a purpose.
   b. It is possible at certain times of the year.
   c. It is characteristic of many peoples in the world.

d. It was practiced only by people who moved from place to place.

e. It is the most accurate way to mark seasonal changes.

3. The constellation Dilyehe

a. rises in the Northeast at 10 p.m. near the autumn equinox.

b. is absent from the night sky near the time of the summer equinox.

c. is not present near the autumn equinox in September.

d. appears not far after the first autumn frost.

e. rises in the morning sky when it is time to plant and harvest.

4. According to the passage, the ancient Navajos left little physical evidence of their knowledge of astronomy because their

a. stargazing equipment was often lost during seasonal migration.

b. calendar was constructed of perishable materials.

c. observations were not dependent on permanent structures.

d. calendar was developed only recently in their history.

e. method of astronomical observation varied with each generation.

5. The author would most likely agree with which of the following statements about the Pueblo calendar?

a. It relies heavily on the position of the Sun as well as on that of the stars.

b. It depends on the Sun's position relative to fixed dwellings.

c. It makes seasonal calculations of the Sun's position unnecessary.

d. It requires that the position of the sun be calculated by several Sun chiefs.

e. It is checked against time markers determined by sightings of certain constellations.

6. The author probably wanted readers to agree with the following statement.

a. The Navajos had a more useful calendar than the Pueblos did.

b. The Pueblos were less adventurous than the Navajos were.

c. The Navajos and the Pueblos had different lifestyles which were reflected in their calendars.

d. The Navajos probably knew how to plant and harvest their crops in a better way than the Pueblos did.

e. The stars are a more useful standard for constructing a calendar than the Sun and Moon are.

Appendix B: Note-Taking Strategies Assessment

Student _____   Level_____ Date_____

Note-taking Strategies Assessment version .6 (c) Vann & Schmidt, 1992				
STRATEGY	**NO**	**YES**	**NUMBER**	**est. % of all notes (optional)**
1.TRANSLATION				
2.DEFINITION				
3. HIGHLIGHTING UNDERLINING				
a. vocabulary				
b. main ideas				
c. details				
4. LISTS				
a. vocabulary				
b. main ideas				
5. DIAGRAMMING				
a. math symbols				
b. pictures				
c. words				
d. outlining				
6. COPYING				
7. PARAPHRASING				
a. telegraphic				
b. sentences				
8. MISPHRASING				

Translation= *any unit or set of characters written in another language & separated by white space.*

Definition= *the meaning of a word or phrase written in English.*

Highlighting *= using a colored marker or otherwise marking (includes underlining.)*
  vocab *= highlighting or underlining a single word or idiom.*
  main ideas *= highlighting or underlining topic sentences or sub-topic.*
  details *= highlighting or underlining other information (a unit = anything separated by white space.*

List *= a group of items written in vertical columns.*

Diagram *= graphic devices including linking or separating lines, parentheses or brackets, space to separate concepts, arrows, bullets, footnotes.*

Copying *= word for word transcription from the original document*

Paraphrasing *= restating text in another form or other words.*
  Telegraphic *= key words are written and function words omitted.*
  Sentences *= whole sentences are used.*

Misphrasing *= distortion of original meaning.*

Appendix C: Recall Protocol

RECALL PROTOCOL .3 (C) SCHMIDT & VANN
NAVAJO AND PUEBLO CALENDARS

Student _____   Level _____   Date _____

P	P= Present 1= Importance Rating (1-4)*
1	Navajos/Pueblos calendars different
1	Differences reflected in celestial motions for reckoning calendar
1	Navajos used stars for calendar
1	Pueblos used sun (and moon) for calendar
2	Navajo-star calendar useful for mobile lifestyle /fixed position of stars/methods could be carried in memory to many locations
2	Pueblo sun-calendar useful for living in one place year-round /fixed horizon and fixed place/position of own pueblo
3	Navajos derived livelihood primarily from ranching /sheep/cattle herders
3	Navajos moved from place to place
3	Navajos also agriculturists/tilled soil
2	Navajos used constellation Dilyehe
3	Dilyehe = one illustration of how Navajos used stars as calendar markers
4	Dilyehe rises at summer solstice
4	Dilyehe useful calendar throughout the world
4	Dilyehe appears in (N.E.) morning sky after several months absence
4	Dilyehe tells when too late to plant and still be able to harvest before first frost
4	Late Sept. near autumn equinox (10 P.M.) Dilyehe rises in (N.E)
4	Dilyehe tells first autumn not far off
4	Dilyehe = clock (during fall and winter nights)
3	Archaeologists noted ancient Pueblos left structures/windows placed at certain angles oriented toward sun
3	Archaeologists noted ancient Navajos left little physical evidence /needed no fixed cues
	TOTAL IDEAS RECALLED
	AVERAGE IMPORTANCE LEVEL OF IDEAS RECALLED

*1 = most central ideas; 4 = most detailed ideas

Distortions of ideas or personal opinions:

Appendix D: Strategies Checklist

Directions: Use the checkmarks on your Note-Taking Strategies Assessment sheet to help you answer the following questions.

Efficient Strategies

1. I did not translate. (No. 1)
2. I focused on main ideas. (Nos. 3b, 4b)
3. I structured ideas by diagramming. (No. 5)
4. I paraphrased (used some of my own words). (No. 7)
5. I did not distort the meaning (took accurate notes). (No. 8)

Inefficient Strategies

1. I translated. (No. 1)
2. I focused on details (No. 3c) and/or vocabulary. (Nos. 2, 3a, 4a)
3. I did not diagram. (No. 5)
4. I copied word-for-word. (No. 6)
5. I misphrased (distorted the original meaning). (No. 8)

Contributors

Helen Hoyt Schmidt is an instructor in the Intensive English and Orientation Program at Iowa State University, where she teaches advanced reading and composition. Roberta Vann is Associate Professor at Iowa State University, where she teaches in the Master's Program in TESL.

Developing a Course for Nurses

Levels
High intermediate +

Aims
Read authentic texts for main ideas and important details
Use this information to answer questions in the reading class
Perform classroom tasks related to nursing
Understand the answers to Operation Nightingale practice examinations

Class Time
2 hours

Preparation Time
2 hours

Resources
Nursing school textbooks and professional journals

Nursing students must be able to read assigned texts efficiently and to recall and use the information to finish a review course and pass the National Council for Licensure Exam for Registered Nurses (NCLEX-RN). These activities come from materials developed for Operation Nightingale, a 14-week intensive review course for international Registered Nurses who are preparing for the NCLEX-RN in Honolulu, Hawaii. However, the skills focus of the activities can be applied to other English for science and technology situations.

Procedures

Selecting and Ordering the Units

1. Working with content experts (i.e., other faculty members who teach the students' content courses), select a number of thematic units the students will need to study during the session. The length of the units will vary depending on the curriculum and the students' needs.
2. Begin with texts on familiar topics. These texts should be short to focus attention on the skills you are teaching rather than on new content.
3. Try to schedule the more advanced, longer, or more difficult texts in the middle of the session. Work with the other instructors to avoid conflicts, fitting your curriculum to theirs as much as possible so that your students are reading either texts that have been assigned in their other classes or texts that will help them with the content load of those classes in some way.
4. End your class session with topics with which the students are familiar or which recycle or review content taught during the session. Don't save the most difficult texts for the last.

Preparing and Teaching a Unit

1. Select a number of related articles or textbook chapters that deal with the theme of the unit. Be sure to select current material that is appropriate for the students in your class and that is well written (i.e., ideas are clearly presented and easy to follow; charts and graphs are understandable and useful for interpreting the text; text is easy to photocopy; type is large enough; photographs will copy well; subtitles, glosses, and footnotes help break up the text in a comprehensible manner).

2. Order the texts so that ideas and specific vocabulary are introduced in the first part of the unit and are presented in different contexts in later readings.

3. Read the articles yourself, underlining main ideas and important details. Make lots of margin notes. Be sure that you understand the text. Identify technical and general vocabulary the students should know in order to understand the main ideas and details or to answer any questions you will develop for the worksheets or examinations. Don't get sidetracked, as students sometimes do, with extraneous vocabulary items that only appear once or twice in the texts and are used to explain an aside or unimportant details.

4. Develop worksheets for each class session. You may want to do a separate worksheet for each text or a worksheet that requires students to work across texts (i.e., use more than one to answer the questions). The prereading and comprehension activities (and any homework or follow up activities) should be copied separately so that students focus on one activity at a time. The text should also be separate so that students can put together a folio of authentic texts for use in other classes.

Typical Operation Nightingale Class Activities

1. Prereading exercises or discussion may require students to complete a chart or graph, discuss two or three main ideas with a partner, answer general questions about the topic, predict the content of the text using the title, demonstrate knowledge of useful vocabulary by

explaining the term(s) in their own words in English, make a drawing of a system by themselves or with a partner, or do any other activity that stimulates thinking about the topic.

2. Vocabulary in context exercises come from sentences in the text that contain vocabulary necessary for comprehension of main ideas or important details. These sentences may be highlighted on the students' copies of the text or retyped on separate worksheet pages; vocabulary word(s) are underlined. If the vocabulary is given as a prereading exercise, students explain the meaning of some terms in their own words in English or, if they all have the same first language and we understand it, give the equivalent in their first language. Vocabulary is also presented as part of the comprehension activities, or as a handout. We try not to spend too much class time on terminology because vocabulary is a tool, not the main focus of the class.

3. Reading is done in class so that the students develop new reading skills while we monitor the process. They skim through the text first in order to get an idea of its length and organization, then they read. We model the process we want them to acquire.

4. We allow dictionary use, but limit it. We suggest that students circle or underline words or terms they don't understand, try to guess their meaning in context first, or keep reading to see if the term is explained later in the text.

5. Some students will finish early and some won't finish on time; when a majority of the class has finished reading, distribute the comprehension worksheets. Students can also request the worksheet or come to your desk for it when they finish reading (if classroom size, arrangement, number of students, etc., will allow this without disturbing the students who are still reading). If some students consistently finish very early, have extra readings available for them. Be sure students who read very slowly are included in the follow-up activities by calling on them for the first few comprehension answers.

6. Allow at least 30–45 minutes for students to write the answers and 20–30 minutes for discussion of the answers. Cover the main points, but don't write so many questions that students can't finish them in the allotted time (12–15 per session for 12–13 pages of text: students summarize answers in their own words as much as possible). Don't

give the questions in the same order in which the information is presented in the text; make students scan the text to answer the questions. Vary the type of comprehension activities. If the text doesn't contain a chart, have students complete one. Include illustrations that need to be labeled. If your class is small enough, students can perform role plays to demonstrate their understanding of key points or they can explain a procedure to the class. Try to include more application and analysis questions than display questions. Work with content teachers to develop real-world tasks which require students to use the information in the texts to perform the tasks. Comprehension questions can also be given as a prereading activity; students answer as many questions as possible before they see the text, then they add information to their answers as they read.

Caveats and Options

Many instructors are not experts in the content areas they teach but can become experts on the texts they teach. Inform yourself about the content area as much as possible. Also, students are themselves experts in their own fields (or are on the way to becoming experts). Reminding them and yourself of this fact increases their self-confidence and autonomy.

Contributor

Shira J. Smith teaches at Operation Nightingale, Honolulu, Hawaii. She received her MA in TESOL, with Distinction, from Monterey Institute of International Studies, California, in 1986.

◆ Reading Rate
Pump It Up

Levels
Intermediate +

Aims
Increase reading rate

Class Time
5–10 minutes

Preparation Time
15 minutes

Resources
Whatever text students
are using

Rapid reading techniques prepare students to read fluently by getting them away from reading word-by-word. One advantage of this reading rate activity is that an entire class can be reading the same text or individual readers may be reading material that has been self-selected.

Procedure

1. Give students 1 minute to read as much material as they can in a text. Time them.
2. After a minute, tell them to stop and write the number 1 where they are in the text.
3. Then have the students return to the beginning of the passage and read again for another minute.
4. After the second minute, have them write the number 2 where they are in the text. The goal is to read more material in the second minute than in the first.
5. Repeat this procedure a third and fourth time. Each time have the students record the number (1, 2, 3, or 4) so that comparisons can be made for each minute-long period.

Caveats and Options

Because reading rates can vary greatly from student to student, comparisons should not be made between two students. Progress can be measured as students evaluate their own reading performances.

References and Further Reading

Anderson, N. J. (1986, October). Increasing the reading rate of ESL students. *TESOL Newsletter*, p. 8.

Contributor

Neil J. Anderson is Assistant Professor in the Department of Linguistics at Ohio University. His research interests include second language reading and testing.

Repeated Reading

Levels
Intermediate +

Aims
Increase reading rate
and comprehension of
second language readers

Class Time
5–10 minutes

Preparation Time
15 minutes

Resources
Whatever text students
are using

Readers build reading fluency and learn to process text more efficiently when they reread. Samuels (1979) states that the repeated reading technique "emerged largely from the teaching implications of the theory of automatic information processing in reading. According to automaticity theory, a fluent reader decodes text automatically—that is, without attention—thus leaving attention free to be used for comprehension. . . . One important function of repeated reading is that it provides the practice needed to become automatic" (p. 406).

Procedure

1. Select a passage from the text assigned for the class with comprehension questions already prepared. Prepare questions for special reading materials used in class.
2. Have students reread a short passage over and over until they achieve criterion levels of reading rate and comprehension. The criterion levels may vary from class to class or student to student. Goals to work towards are criterion levels of 200 words-per-minute with at least 75% comprehension.

Caveats and Options

Teachers can set a criterion level for a class or, better yet, students can set their own criterion level and focus on improvement of reading fluency without a particular emphasis on testing reading comprehension.

References and Further Reading

Samuels, S. J. (1979). The method of repeated readings. *The Reading Teacher, 32*, 403-408.

Contributor

Neil J. Anderson is Assistant Professor in the Department of Linguistics at Ohio University. His research interests include second language reading and testing.

Developing Metalinguistic Reading Skills

Levels
Low intermediate

Aims
Practice eye traveling along the boundaries of subject, verb, and object of sentences, recognizing and relating their meanings

Class Time
25–30 minutes

Preparation Time
10–15 minutes

Resources
A paragraph or two from newspapers, magazines, or texts

Few L2 students have been trained to utilize reading strategies that are frequently used by native speakers. These two activities are effective in developing comprehension and speed in reading.

Procedure

1. Have student pairs locate the main verb or verb phrase, subject, and object of each sentence in the paragraph and underline them.
2. Take turns practicing eye traveling by reading alternating sentences in the paragraph *aloud*, pausing at the end of the identified subject, verb, and object clusters.
3. Ask each pair to read the passage *silently* for comprehension and to decide that the main idea of the paragraph is.
4. Ask the pairs to discuss, check their comprehension, and prepare to answer your questions.

Caveats and Options

Have subsequent paragraphs include sentences that are longer and more complicated.

Contributor

Penny L. Cefola received her PhD in Applied Linguistics from Georgetown University. She is Associate Professor of Linguistics and ESL at California Lutheran University and has taught linguistics and EFL in Korea and Thailand.

Speed Reading

Levels
Any

Aims
Increase reading speed

Skill
Scanning

Class Time
10–20 minutes

Preparation Time
5 minutes (if the students' text includes comprehension questions and the teacher's manual includes an answer key)

Resources
Class set of a previously unread text
One answer key for every several learners

Many learners, especially those who have studied English through grammar/translation, read far too slowly to process meaning. Also, many students don't consider the purpose of their reading and, as a result, often don't understand much of what they read. This activity increases their awareness by having them focus on the questions to be answered before they read. It also builds speed by teaching students to scan for particular information.

Procedure

1. Have learners turn the reading passage face down on their desks.
2. Tell them that this is a speed reading activity and that you will ask each question twice to make sure everyone understands. When you tell them to start, they should turn over the text and look for the answer as quickly as possible. When they find it, they should call out the answer.
3. Do the first two or three questions as indicated in Step 2. When a student answers, have that person show the other the location of the information in the text. Once they understand the procedure, move on to Step 4.
4. Divide the class into groups of four or five. In each group, one person is the "quizmaster." That person gets a copy of the answer sheet. Quizmasters take over your role from Step 2. They ask the questions (twice!). Then members of their groups compete to find the answers. (The quizmasters clarify with you any questions about which they're unsure.)

Caveats and Options

1. If students are answering at the same time, have them put an eraser or other object in the middle the group. It represents a "game show

buzzer." Learners must touch the buzzer before they can answer. The problem of who was first is solved because the hand on the buzzer will indicate the fastest person.

2. Rotate the role of quizmaster: The person who answers a question correctly becomes quizmaster for the next one.

3. If students have a difficult time understanding the questions at Step 2 and are unused to clarifying what they hear, have everyone stand. Read the question. Students can sit down once they understand the question either from your reading it or from asking you for clarification or repetition. Wait until everyone is seated before starting.

4. This activity works best with literal comprehension questions. Although such questions represent only one level of testing understanding, they are the most common type in many textbooks. Also, begin with questions about the general meaning of the passage so students have an overall understanding before focusing on specifics.

Contributors

Marc Helgesen teaches at Miyagi Gakuin, Sendai, Japan. He is the co-author of several ESL texts, including English Firsthand, New English Firsthand, *and* New English Firsthand Plus. *Don Maybin teaches at the Language Institute of Japan, Odawara, Japan.*

Reading Relay

Levels
Any

Aims
Give readers a purpose
for reading and
encourage them to
share their knowledge
of a reading passage

Class Time
30–45 minutes

Preparation Time
30 minutes

Resources
Reading passages from
students' reading text
or from other sources

In this activity, which focuses on speed reading, skimming, and scanning skills, students compete against a clock—but not against one another. If you have not done cooperative learning activities in the class before, you might want to introduce the concept of cooperative learning before you try this activity.

Procedure

1. Divide the reading passage into easy-to-read parts. The students work in groups, so make sufficient sets for the number of students in the class. For example, if you have 12 students and the story has three parts, make four sets.
2. Make up any kind of comprehension questions you wish for the entire reading passage.
3. Divide the students into small groups. The number of students in each group should equal the number of reading parts you have in each set.
4. Explain the activity. Each member of the group receives a different part of the reading. They read that part as many times as they can before the signal. At the signal, the students pass the reading passage to the student on their right. This continues until each student has had an opportunity to read each part of the passage.
5. Hand out the reading to each group. Tell the students to start reading as you begin to time them. The length of time you let the students read depends on their ability and how much you want to focus on skimming skills and reading speed.
6. After the students have finished reading all the parts of the reading, collect them and give each group one copy of the comprehension questions. As the students to work as a group to answer the questions.

7. Give each student the entire reading and go over the comprehension questions.

Contributor

Katharine Isbell is the Program Developer and an instructor for the Asahi Chemical Industry Co. employee English program in Nobeoka, Japan. Previously, she was a teacher trainer in Thailand and Indonesia.

Increasing Reading Speed

Levels
Intermediate

Aims
Heighten awareness of
students' reading speeds
and then increase them

Class Time
30 minutes

Preparation Time
10–30 minutes

Resources
Lesson from *An
American Sampler*,
American Patterns,
American Vistas, or
another short passage
Reading speed chart
Time record chart
Watch with a second
hand

It is important to be able to read passages quickly to understand the main ideas. When readers process a text too slowly, they cannot absorb meaning fully and may only be able to process individual words.

Reading Rate Chart

Procedure

1. Choose an easy passage 300–1,500 words long, depending on the students' reading proficiency.
2. Draw the figure below on the blackboard:

Minutes	Seconds
0	30
10	40
20	50

3. Ask the students to start reading. While timing the reading, point at the seconds and write in the numbers of the minutes. When the students finish reading, tell them to look up to see their times.
4. Have students write their times on the time record chart, if they are using textbooks with one, or on a chart that they make up if they are not. They should use the reading speed chart to find out how

many words/minute they are reading and record this information on the time record chart. (Students can also calculate reading speed by dividing the number of words in the passage by the time spent reading.)

Caveats and Options

This technique should be used over a period of time. It makes students aware of their reading speed and how it is improving. The technique is, of course, used in conjunction with exercises related to reading comprehension.

References and Further Reading

Kitao, K. et al. (1983). *An American sampler*. Reading, MA: Addison-Wesley.

Kitao, K. et al. (1985). *American patterns*. Reading, MA: Addison-Wesley.

Kitao, K. et al. (1985). *American vistas*. Reading, MA: Addison-Wesley.

Contributor

Kenji Kitao is a co-author of 25 textbooks and of Intercultural Communication: Between Japan and the United States.

◆ Literature
Making Stories Their Own

Levels
Intermediate +;
elementary

Aims
Practice reading for
comprehension
Provide different ways
for students to respond
to literature

Class Time
45–60 minutes

Preparation Time
15 minutes

Resources
Ethnic folktales,
legends, and realistic
stories

When students engage in activities requiring them to reread stories, their understanding at the literal and interpretive levels improves greatly. Ethnic folktales, legends, and other stories make rereading enjoyable.

Procedure

1. Pictomap. After they read or listen to a story, ask students to

   - draw a map identifying where major scenes took place
   - retell what happened at each place
   - cut out circles to draw the episodes as inset pictures
   - glue pictures onto the map
   - draw arrows to indicate event sequence.

   They can go back to the story at any point of the project. This activity works well with adventure stories. Structures covered include sequence and cause-effect.

2. Point-of-view. Using a talk show format, have students take on the roles of guests and host. As they work together to plan for questions and answers, encourage students to express their feelings and viewpoints as though they were the real characters. This activity allows students to understand a story from an insider's point of view. It also enables students to consider values and interpretations of events as they consider various perspectives. Role play during the actual presentation time is a wonderful opportunity for ESL students to play with ways of speaking.

3. Mural. Ask students to create a definite scene that best represents the story. It is necessary to emphasize careful reading or library

research if necessary to get the details right. The main thrust of the project is to interpret the *tone* and *mood* of the story. Students can experience how to create desirable effects using different media, such as paint, chalk, finger paint, and three-dimensional paper art. (Use dark paper as background; avoid white.)

4. Sculpture. Give clay to students to create a solid symbol for the story. It is important to have two or three students work together because through discussion, they can come up with a theme or underlying message of the story. After the sculpture is done, they need to explain orally or in written form how their sculpture is a symbol for the story.

Recommended Booklist

Adams, E. B. (1982). *Korean Cinderella*. Seoul, Korea: Seoul International Publishing House. (Korean folktale)

Bunting, E. (1988). *How many days to America: A Thanksgiving story*. New York: Clarion Books. (Caribbean island story)

Fuentes, V. M. A. (1989). *Pearl makers*. New York: Friendship Press.

Galdone, P. (1983). *The turtle and the monkey*. New York: Clarion Books. (Filipino tale)

Kidd, D. (1989). *Onion tears*. New York: Orchard Books. (Vietnamese story)

Kurusa, K. (1985). *The streets are free*. Scarborough, Ontario: Firefly Books. (Venezuelan story)

Levine, E. (1989). *I hate English*. New York: Scholastic. (Chinese story)

Livo, N. J., & Cha, D. (1991). *Folk tales of the Hmong*. Englewood, CO: Libraries Unlimited. (Hmong folktales)

Louie, A. (1982). *Yeh-Shen: A Cinderella story from China*. New York: Philomel. (Chinese folktale)

Shute, L. (1986). *Momotaro: The peach boy*. New York: Lothrop, Lee & Shepard Books. (Japanese folktale)

Terada, A. M. (1989). *Under the starfruit tree: Folktales from Vietnam*. Honolulu: University of Hawaii Press. (Vietnamese folktales)

Contributor

Belinda Yun-Ying Louie is Assistant Professor of Education at the University of Washington, Tacoma, where she teaches children's and young adult literature, reading, and language arts.

What's the Ending?

Levels
Intermediate +

Aims
Integrate listening, speaking, and writing with the reading of a short story
Give students the opportunity to interpret literature through individual cultural perspectives and compare these perspectives with those of their classmates and the author(s)

Class Time
Two classes, 1 hour each

Preparation Time
No set time

Resources
A short story, preferably one with a surprise ending

Students can discover that meaning in literature is not fixed and that cultural background and individual experience affect both the writing and interpretation of literature. According to the skills development you want to emphasize, the steps in this approach can be varied to include oral presentations and additional reading, writing, and collaborative activities.

Procedure

1. Make copies of the story, omitting the ending.
2. Introduce the title and author and have students work in pairs or groups to predict what the story will be about. Direct a discussion in which you provide cultural and other background information necessary for basic comprehension of the story.
3. Pass out photocopies of the story and ask students to read it silently. Do not tell students the ending is missing.
4. Conduct a whole-class discussion of the story. Give attention to problems of vocabulary, colloquial language, and idiomatic expressions, but keep the focus on meaning. This discussion should be lively because students will have recognized that the story was incomplete.
5. Ask students to reread the story as homework and to write individual versions of the story's conclusion. Encourage them to include dialogue.
6. In the next class, have students share their compositions with a partner or group.
7. Pass out the texts and instruct students to read the author's ending silently.
8. Conduct a whole-class discussion comparing the author's ending with the students' endings. Discuss the entire story, focusing on how cul-

tural differences influenced both the students' writing and their comprehension of the story.

Caveats and Options

1. If it is not possible to make copies, or texts are not available, read the chosen story aloud. In this case, the story should be as short as possible and students should be encouraged to take notes during the reading (see Step 3, above).
2. If the class is small and time is available, students can read their conclusions aloud to the class or present them as role plays with other students (see Step 6, above).
3. Even if texts are available, you may choose to read the ending of the story aloud for listening practice and to pass out the texts later (see Step 7, above).
4. For extended writing practice, students can work through an additional draft, or drafts, of their composition.

Contributor

Ellen McGill has taught ESL/EFL for more than 10 years in the United States, Japan, and Guatemala. She is the co-author of Understanding Computers, Computers in the Office, *and* Computers for Businesspeople, *all published by Heinle and Heinle.*

Group Literature Reading

Levels
Advanced

Aims
Explore understanding
of literature
Develop critical
thinking skills

Class Time
30–50 minutes per
week

Preparation Time
1 hour per week

Resources
Five to six full length
literary works

Most nonnative speaking students have not had any background in reading full-length works of literature in English. Yet these works provide vocabulary, sentence patterns, writing styles, and ideas which can enhance their use of English. With guided interaction with literature, students can gain the interest and confidence to pursue reading longer literary works on their own.

Procedure

1. Introduce selected works to the class; ask students to choose books by lottery system, creating groups of four to five students per book.
2. Allowing approximately 4 weeks to complete reading, have groups set up their own schedule of reading and division of labor for oral presentation (see Appendix below).
3. Each week, Have groups meet for discussion and have each student hand in a personal reading response journal.
4. Ask that group oral reports be given at which time students should hand in individual written reports.

Caveats and Options

1. Give this assignment the second half of the course after the class has read a novel together and written an essay on it. Although this rather independent assignment is not easy for the students, it encourages them to pursue the reading of full-length pieces of literature on their own.
2. Near the end of the course, give students a limited recommended reading list. Students can succeed at different levels of competency with this assignment.

Appendix: Group Literature Reading

Directions: A small group of classmates will read the same novel or biographical work and discuss it in and out of class. Each student will keep a weekly response journal based on the group's weekly reading assignment. As a group, they will plan and present a group report (30 minutes) to the class about the book they read. Each member of the group will hand in a short report (two typed pages) on his/her portion of the group presentation.

The books are as follows:

When Heaven and Earth Changed Places, by Le Ly Hayslip
Typical American, by Gish Jen
Hunger of Memory, by Richard Rodriguez
Iron and Silk, by Mark Salzman
The Education of Harriet Hatfield, by May Sarton
Black Boy, by Richard Wright

Ideas for Group Discussion and Response Journal

Setting:
What is the time and place of the book?
What is the mood of the book?

Characters:
Name and describe the characters.
Are there main characters and minor ones?
What are the relationships among the characters?
Are there characters who are opponents—good against evil?
Compare and contrast the characters if appropriate.

Plot:
Summarize the events of the book.
Is there a conflict or conflicts between:
two people?
a person and his/her conscience (internal)?
a person and society?
a person and an animal or nature?

Structure and Style (how the story is told):

Is there a narrator (an outsider telling the story)?

Is the book written in the first or third person (I or he/she)?

Does the book move back and forth in time?

Is there humor, irony, symbolism, metaphors?

Is there any special language used? (dialects, foreign words, slang)

Themes:

What is the main idea or author's message? (usually it is a generalization about life, society, people's behavior or attitudes)

Personal Responses:

What is your reaction to the story or theme or to a character?

What are your feelings and thoughts based on what you read?

Can you relate anything you read to yourself or real life?

Did you learn anything from the book?

Choose a phrase or sentence that attracts you and explain why it does.

The above questions are meant to stimulate thinking and group discussion. Group members do not have to answer all of these nor report on all of these. However, the group presentation should touch on these matters and include the interesting ideas from the group's discussions. In the group presentation, each individual is a speaker for the group and may present ideas from any group member which came up during group discussions. In the individual report, each student should summarize his portion of the group's presentation.

Listener Participation

After each group presentation, the class will ask questions about the book and about what was presented. Class discussion on topics concerning the book will follow each presentation. Constructive comments and criticism about the presentation are also welcome at this time.

Group Grading Criteria

The following will be considered for an overall grade:

Did the group present their material in an integrated related way? (not as separate unrelated reports but as a connected whole)

Did they present the material in an organized way?
Were they easily understood? (slow, clear, loud, careful pronunciation)
Were they well-prepared? (not reading from paper and working well together as if they had practiced together?)
Was the content of the presentation interesting, informative, insightful?

Overall Grading

5% for weekly response journals (2 handwritten blue book pages/week)
10% for group presentation (30 minutes)
5% for written report (2 typed pages, double spaced)

Written reports are due on the assigned day of your group presentation. Journals are due weekly.

Contributor

Claudine Poggi has been teaching ESL since 1976. Affiliated with DeAnza College in Cupertino, California, she has presented at TESOL and California TESOL (CATESOL) conferences and contributes to CATESOL publications.

Reading Poetry: The Sonnet

Levels
Intermediate +

Aims
Practice reading for
sound and main ideas
Introduce another style
of reading matter

Class Time
45 minutes

Preparation Time
30 minutes

Resources
A sonnet, one copy per
student
Worksheet, one copy
per student

Poetry is often neglected in ESL programs. The introduction of this material will motivate some students to read more of it. This activity is especially appropriate for students of English for academic purposes, but it can be used for variety in other programs.

Procedure

1. Pass out copies of the sonnet. Ask the students to underline unfamiliar word as you read the sonnet aloud.
2. Pass out the worksheet (see Appendix below). Invite the students to complete as much of the worksheet as possible in the following 20 minutes.
3. Have the class compare their answers.
4. Follow up with other sonnets and then introduce other types of English literature.

Appendix: Worksheet for Reading a Sonnet

Every good sonnet is a poem that shares certain characteristics. You don't need to understand every word to complete this worksheet, but notice the following:

1. How many lines does the sonnet have?
2. Do the lines rhyme?

Write the last word of the first line in Blank A. Then write the last word of any line that sounds the same as the word in Blank A in the next blanks:

A. _____ _____ _____
   _____ _____ _____

Write the last word of the second line in Blank B. Then write the last word of any line that sounds the same a the word in Blank B in the next blanks:

B. _____ _____ _____
   _____ _____ _____

3. Does the poem have meter? Count the syllables in each line. Place an accent over the syllables that should be stressed.
4. Does the poem have visual imagery? Circle each of the words in the poem that suggest a picture.
5. Write one sentence summarizing the poem's main idea.

Contributor

Hugh Rutledge graduated from Boston University. He has taught in East Asia for 4 years and is Head of Faculty at Tokyo International College, Japan.

Stage Play

Levels
Intermediate +;
preacademic

Aims
Offer background
knowledge to
understand the plot,
situations, and
characters in an
American literary work
Acquire a better
understanding of a
particular facet of
American culture

Class Time
1–2 hours

Preparation Time
15–20 minutes

Resources
Any novel or short
story that students have
already read

Role play is useful in teaching and reinforcing material introduced through fiction, for which nonnative students often have only a limited schema. For this activity, students act out and expand on a dialogue in the text. In this way, they have a chance to reinforce the knowledge they have acquired previously through more traditional activities, such as answering study questions. Also, they have a chance to understand material that they have had difficulty with. When students do this activity appropriately, they demonstrate an understanding of the material. Students are also actively engaged in processing the material when they can see themselves in it.

Procedure

1. Review with the class one of the dialogues discussed in previous lessons. For example, students could take turns reading aloud. Encourage students to show the proper emotion when they are reading their parts. Ask students to explain why certain emotions might be more appropriate than others when acting out this scene.
2. Divide the class into groups. Tell them that they are to write a portion of a script for a play about the book. Explain that they are to use existing dialogue in the text and that they should expand on this dialogue by carrying through with the ideas or situation in the dialogue. Give them the freedom to choose the passage of text that they would like to act out. Indicate approximately how long their dialogues should be.
3. Have each group perform its dialogue in front of the class. Students could be encouraged to make slight rearrangements in the classroom as they might on a stage set.

Caveats and Options

1. *The Outsiders,* a young adult novel by S. E. Hinton (1967, Bantam Books), is good for this activity. It explores the role of the initiation experience in U.S. culture, the problems of the young adult, and the clash between two subcultures.
2. Have groups choose students from the class (or other students from the same program that most in the class would probably know) who they feel would be appropriate choices to play the characters. For this activity, each group attempts to cast all or most of the major and minor characters. Groups can share their lists with other groups and be prepared to defend the choices they have made.
3. For students who are having trouble getting started, I advise them to, first, choose a passage with dialogue that they like or think is significant. I advise them to copy the existing dialogue in a manner that is similar to dialogues presented in their conversation textbooks. I then ask students questions such as, "Now, if this conversation were longer, what do you think Ponyboy would say?", or, "How would Cherry respond to Ponyboy's question about the sunset?"
4. If students do not want to use existing dialogue, but are able to write an appropriate dialogue entirely on their own, that is also acceptable. The learning goals concern the students' understanding of the cultural situation presented in that particular section of the novel. Instructing students to use existing dialogue is helpful in getting them started on the assignment.
5. Encourage students to make use of any idiomatic expressions that they have learned while studying this text. As students perform their skits, you might step in as director to indicate whether students are showing emotions that are appropriate to the cultural intent of the passage.

Contributor

Michele Slinkard received an MA in EFL from Southern Illinois University. She teaches in a university preparatory program in the United States.

◆ Assessment/Evaluation
Answer the Questions Without the Passage

Levels
Any

Aims
Practice strategies for
taking reading tests

Class Time
25–40 minutes

Preparation Time
30 minutes

Resources
A passage of about 700
words, with 10–12
multiple choice
comprehension
questions

Students practiced in test-taking techniques have a wider variety of coping skills and more confidence than those who are not. This activity can be used with a class of almost any level so long as the passage and questions reflect their reading level. If you repeat the activity several times, it will become evident that some students are much less testwise than others—and should be suitably counseled.

Procedure

1. Select an appropriate reading passage and make one copy for every three to four students.
2. Make enough copies of the questions so that each student has a copy.
3. Divide the class into groups of three or four.
4. Distribute the questions but not the passage.
5. Ask groups to decide on the correct answers without first seeing the passage.
6. Give out the passage when all groups have finished.
7. Have students read the passage and correct their answers.
8. Ask students to reflect on their performance.
9. Have groups explain to the class successful and unsuccessful approaches to particular questions.

Caveats and Options

Include a few free response questions by omitting the alternatives from some of the multiple choice items, rewording the stems where necessary.

Contributor

Alastair Allan is Senior Lecturer in English at the City Polytechnic of Hong Kong. His interests include language proficiency test validation and EFL/ESL reading.

Reading-Portfolio Assessment

Levels
Intermediate +

Aims
Demonstrate students'
reading development
Encourage self-
reflection and self-
assessment by students

Class Time
No set time

Preparation Time
No set time

Resources
Any suitable reading
material

By making decisions about what to include in their reading portfolio and how to organize the contents, students reflect on what they have read and learned. The reading portfolio should include a variety of authentic readings for inside and outside the classroom. Selection of the content should be a continuous process throughout the semester. Assessment should reflect your collaborative efforts with your students.

Procedure

1. At the beginning of the semester, introduce this new form of assessment.
2. Discuss academic goals, possible reading materials, the standard for evaluation, and the purpose of building individual reading portfolios.
3. Throughout the semester, ask students to accumulate selectively their reading journals, summaries of articles, newspaper reports, classroom reading exercises, and any reading outside the classroom into their portfolios.
4. Respond to the entries in the portfolios and discuss the contents periodically.
5. At the end of the semester, ask students to reorganize the materials in their portfolios and divide them into meaningful sections. Ask students to write a brief summary reflecting on and evaluating their progress during the semester.
6. Ask students to present their reading portfolios orally.

Caveats and Options

For intermediate-level students, you can assign reading summaries as regular homework and demonstrate what a reading journal is like. For advanced students, you should encourage independent reading in real-life situations.

Contributor

Jian Zhang is Assistant Professor of Reading and ESL at Suffolk Community College, Brentwood, New York. He is the author of Living English for Native Chinese Speakers, *to be published by Crown Publishing in 1993.*

◆ Vocabulary
List, Group, Label (and Write)

Levels
Advanced; preacademic

Aims
Develop independence
in vocabulary building
Encourage students to
categorize new words
into semantically
related groups
Encourage use of
monolingual English
dictionaries

Class Time
Two nonconsecutive
class periods

Preparation Time
45 minutes–1 hour

Resources
Any material students
are currently reading

Students can recall and use more vocabulary if they learn it systematically and independently, that is, without over-reliance on bilingual dictionaries. Learner dictionaries work well if students have not worked with English-English dictionaries before. Discussion is a very important part of this activity. Be prepared for some surprises in the ways students categorize their words.

Procedure

1. Have students read from their regular class text and write down words they do not know. Ask them to choose words from their lists to which they want to pay particular attention. Encourage students to be selective and limit themselves to 5–10 new words per passage.
2. Ask them to use English-only dictionaries, looking up the words they want to learn, and writing the definitions on separate cards. They should also copy the sentence in which the word was found, along with the title of the passage and the page number. If a word has more than one meaning, students should only write the definition that fits the context. This list should be started in class but can be completed as homework.
3. Collect the word cards from the students and compile all the words into a list. This list should include each word, its definition, and the sentence or sentences showing its context. The same sentence may come up several times, with different words being selected as new vocabulary. If this occurs, include sentences preceding or following in the paragraph to supply additional contextual information.
4. Have students, working alone or in pairs, put the words into categories that include words with similar meanings and connection to a similar general topic or concept. Opposites can be placed within the same

group. Note that some words will fit into more than one category, and some words will not fit into any category. Tell students *not* to classify words alphabetically or on the basis of parts of speech.

5. Have students give each group of words a label or title that reflects the concept of the category.

6. If students worked alone, have them work in pairs to compare their categories. Ask some pairs to put their categories and labels on the board. Try to choose examples that put the same word into different categories. This can generate some lively discussion about word meanings.

7. Have students explain the groups they made and ask questions about their classmates' categories. If possible, have them explain the relationships they see among words in a group.

Caveats and Options

1. After the initial activities, students can build their own lists or collections of categories. These sets of categories will grow and change as new words are incorporated. Students should review their lists systematically and can be requested to write summaries or essays using words from their lists.

2. Try the grouping step yourself before assigning it to the students, so you can have some models to help the class get started.

Contributors

Marcia Z. Buell and James G. Buell have taught English in Japan, China, the United States and, most recently, Hungary. Their research interests include linking ESL study and testing to academic preparation.

Supply the Phrase

Levels
Intermediate +

Aims
Practice recognition of
context and idiom
Practice reading from
authentic texts

Class Time
40 minutes

Preparation Time
40 minutes

Resources
Paragraphs from
newspapers, magazines,
textbooks, books of
stories

Caveats and Options

Contributor

Students need to have a thorough comprehension of the text to differentiate between vocabulary words that fit in context and those that do not. It is also important for them to be able to recognize if vocabulary is idiomatically appropriate in context. This activity is best for practicing, not introducing vocabulary work.

Procedure

1. Find suitable paragraphs from a variety of sources (e.g., newspapers, magazines, manuals) so that students can practice reading different writing styles.
2. Remove short phrases (most often, no more than two to four words) that suit the context and the structure, and list them on a separate piece of paper. Also add to the list extra short phrases.
3. Divide the class into groups of three to five. Distribute the paragraphs and the fill-ins. Students should be warned that some fill-ins are extra, and do not suit any of the paragraphs.
4. Students should work on all the matchings individually. When the class is ready, check if there is consensus or if more than one answer is possible or best and why.

1. Rather than merely deleting short phrases, supply wrong phrases so that students are required not only to supply a correct phrase but also to recognize where wrong phrases have been placed.
2. You should model activity as you introduce it.

Doris Zames Fleischer received an MA from Teachers College, Columbia University, and a PhD from New York University. She teaches humanities courses at the New Jersey Institute of Technology.

Without a Dictionary

Levels
Low intermediate

Aims
Help students realize that interrupting their reading to look in a dictionary when they meet an unfamiliar word is inefficient and impairs comprehension
Enable students to discover the benefits of reading through a text
Facilitate learner autonomy and give self-confidence

Class Time
45 minutes–1 hour

Preparation Time
5 minutes

Resources
Any appropriate short passage

This activity helps learners realize that they are not wholly dependent on a dictionary for finding the meaning of unknown lexical items. They should discover that they could understand the gist of the reading better when their reading was not interrupted; that they could understand the meaning of many words from the context the second time they read it; that by working together with a partner or in a group, they could help each other to better understand a reading passage; and finally, that they were not dependent on a dictionary to derive meaning.

Procedure

1. Have the students

   - read through the text once, underlining the words they don't know, but not stopping to look them up
   - read through the text again checking the underlined words that they can now understand
   - compare their texts and help each other understand words that are still unknown
   - look in their dictionaries for those words they still don't understand, but feel they must know to get meaning from the text.

2. Elicit from the class what they learned about reading and vocabulary from doing this activity.

Contributor

Eloise Pearson Hamatani received an MA in ESL from the University of Hawaii. An active member of the Japan Association of Language Teachers, she served as a co-editor of its monthly newsletter, The Language Teacher, *for a number of years.*

Lexical Relations

Levels
Intermediate +

Aims
Provide students with
universal strategy for
building up reading
vocabulary

Class Time
30 minutes

Preparation Time
No set time

Resources
Nonfiction reading
passages, preferably
topic- or genre-related

Most vocabulary lists accompanying nonfiction reading passages are preselected by a textbook writer or teacher according to various arbitrary and often mysterious criteria of importance, rarity, slang, and difficulty. However, vocabulary building can be taught to intermediate and advanced students so that they can participate in the target vocabulary selection process. Although the activity relies on the lexical relations created by the content and organization of particular texts, its universal character makes the learning of vocabulary from reading passages more semantically systematic.

Procedure

1. Have groups or pairs of students

   - come up with 10–20 important words and phrases (and their meanings) by looking at key locations in the text: title, introduction, conclusion, first sentences of paragraphs, subheadings
   - pool their lists into a class glossary of key words and phrases
   - examine the glossary for words and phrases that are synonyms, antonyms, or hierarchically related words or phrases (e.g., handicapped/disabled; disabled/able-bodied; and handicapped/paraplegic, respectively)
   - look for other words or phrases in the text to connect with vocabulary that does not fit these relational categories and create their own meaningful connections
   - reorganize the glossary into smaller relational lists for further study.

2. Suggest other ways to categorize key words and phrases that are not topic-specific. For example, have students create a list of words and

phrases that implies quantitative evaluation, such as *overwhelmingly*, *considerable*, *little*, *few*, *substantial.*

3. Have students then try to relate the words and phrases into meaningful categories as in Step 1.

Caveats and Options

1. This activity can be followed up by meaningful reinforcement activities. Do not miss an opportunity to point out familiar words with specialized or text-based meanings: For example, *study* can mean *research.*
2. The activity probably works best after students have analyzed a text for overall structure and basic content.
3. It can also be usefully introduced after preview reading or reading the introduction of a long article and reinvoked as more work is done on the text. No word lists should be presented to the learners prior to this procedure.

Contributor

Sally Jacoby has taught courses in and developed materials for ESL/ EFL reading at all levels since 1976.

Reverse Cloze

Levels
Intermediate +

Aims
Encourage students to
think about what they
are reading and focus
on the sense of a
passage

Class Time
45 minutes

Preparation Time
30 minutes

Resources
Extracts from
textbooks, journals,
magazines, newspapers,
fiction, and special
interest materials

Students often complete gap-filling exercises rather mindlessly without considering the sense of either the sentence or the passage involved. Because they need to read for meaning, they need to use the given context, along with their prior knowledge, to help to them interact intelligently with texts.

Procedure

1. Locate suitable extracts, as described above. All students can read the same one.
2. As students read the extract, ask them to underline and block out the words they don't know.
3. Tell students to read each sentence carefully and insert a word they think will make sense in the context.
4. Have students compare notes with a partner and then with other pairs.
5. Match students' suggestions with the original words. Discuss which are acceptable and which are not.

Caveats and Options

1. Present the task initially as a group exercise.
2. Use suitable texts to help students learn technical terminology related to their disciplines.
3. Encourage students to record the new vocabulary items they have learned and to find opportunities to use them so that they will not forget what they've practiced.

Contributor

Carol MacLennan has taught English in New Zealand, China, Macau, and Hong Kong. Her interests include ESL/EFL reading and writing and teacher education.

Prereading Vocabulary Development

Levels
Intermediate +

Aims
Involve the students in
the learning and
teaching of the
vocabulary needed to
understand an assigned
reading

Class Time
50 minutes

Preparation Time
30 minutes

Resources
Any suitable reading

The more the students are directly involved in an activity, the more they will benefit. This activity requires cooperation among the students and holds them responsible for both teaching and learning the vocabulary needed to understand the reading passage.

Procedure

1. Divide the class into small groups.
2. Give each group a handout (see Appendix below) and assign the students a certain section of the reading. All groups should choose a responsible group leader to act as secretary and make sure all group members participate.
3. Have students read over their assigned section, and then, as a group, choose four unfamiliar vocabulary items that are important for understanding the reading. The students should find the dictionary definition that corresponds to the word's usage in the sentence, then fill in the handout as directed.
4. On the board write the following:

Group 1	Group 2	Group 3	Group 4
Word Line	Word Line	Word Line	Word Line

5. When all the groups have completed their handouts, ask one student from each group to write his group's words and the line number in which they are found on the board. The other students should copy the words as they are being written on the board.
6. Go over the pronunciation of the words.
7. Have groups come to the board one by one to present their words. They should read the line from the text in which the word is found, then give the definition of the word as it is used in the sentence.

8. Ask other students to listen carefully and write the definitions, asking for clarification when necessary. When all the groups have finished, the students will have a vocabulary guide to help them read the article on their own.
9. As a final step, test the students. Make up a matching quiz using the words and definitions.

Appendix: Handout

Direction: With your group members, complete the following exercise. You are responsible for paragraphs _____.

1. Vocabulary

Choose four unfamiliar vocabulary words and find the dictionary definitions that correspond to how the words are used in the sentences. You will explain these words to the class.

Word	Line	Definition
1.	( )	
2.	( )	
3.	( )	
4.	( )	

2. Comprehension

Write four comprehension questions (that require a short answer) about the information given in your paragraphs.

1.
2.
3.
4.

3. Summary

On the back of this paper, write a summary (brief notes only) of the information found in your paragraphs. You will present this to the class.

Contributor

Tracy M. Mannon teaches at the University of Neuchatel in Switzerland. She has taught in Beijing, China, and at the University of Delaware.

Supermarket Vocabulary

Levels
Beginning

Aims
Introduce the concept
of levels of
generalization
Expand knowledge of
high frequency
supermarket vocabulary

Class Time
2 hours

Preparation Time
30 minutes

Resources
Food ads in newspapers
Pictures showing
supermarket layout
Overhead projector and
transparencies

This activity introduces supermarket and food vocabulary. Students go on to add containers, amounts, quantities, prepositions to locate food, customers in the store. There is usually a reading about food shopping in most low-level texts, but if the text you are using doesn't have one, this activity can be adapted easily to clothing or other kinds of shopping.

TODAY'S SPECIAL!

Annie's Peaches
$.91/can

Procedure

1. Locate good illustrations of shopping carts, customers, aisles, and departments.
2. Using an overhead or individual handouts, ask students to identify the different parts of a supermarket in the picture.
3. Have students name as many kinds of food as they know. Write these on a clean transparency or on the blackboard. Identify foods that belong together in departments. Write their group names or cluster them together (e.g., tomatoes/vegetables, cheese/dairy).
4. Distribute news ads (weekend or market fliers with color pictures of food are best). Also give students a handout with the departments listed in outline form:

   I. Produce Department
     A. Vegetables
       1. _____
       2. _____

5. Have student pairs find names for fruit, vegetables, meat, and dairy items and list as many as they can under each department. Circulate to help.
6. Display an overhead transparency of the same handout. List the food items as students say them. Omit repeated items, put items into correct categories as necessary, and correct spelling. Allow students to do as much of this as possible with you as the recorder.
7. As a follow-up assignment for homework, give students easy recipes or a simple budget. They must prepare a shopping list for all the ingredients and within their budget. They should also list food items in departments to make shopping easier.

Contributor

Cheryl McKenzie has an MA in Linguistics from San Jose State University. Employed at Studies in American Language, San Jose State University, she has taught all levels and skill areas of ESL.

Word Recognition

Levels
Beginning +

Aims
Practice word
recognition and
discrimination skills
Facilitate automatic
decoding skills

Class Time
2–5 minutes

Preparation Time
30 minutes

Resources
Material the class has
been reading recently

Through a large number of encounters with any given word, an L1 reader develops automatic and efficient decoding skills. L2 readers, because they do not encounter words with the same frequency as L1 readers, do not usually develop such skills. Even advanced learners are sometimes hampered by a laborious decoding process. However, because fast and automatic decoding skills are necessary for efficient reading, it is important that L2 readers have the opportunity to practice this skill at all levels.

Procedure

1. Choose 10–15 target words, that is, new words that the class has come across recently.
2. For each target word, find a number of distracters (i.e., words that are similar to it, but are not identical). If the target word is a noun, include the plural; if it is a verb, include some inflected forms. Find other words that might be confused with the target word, either visually or aurally.
3. Type each target word on a separate line. Beneath it, type the target words together with a number of distracters.
4. In class, distribute a copy of the exercise to each student and ask students to locate the target word in each line as quickly as they can.

Caveats and Options

1. For beginners, the target words and the distracters should be defined by numbers of letters, and only one target word should be put among the distracters. For intermediate or advanced learners, the procedure could be made progressively more difficult. Possible ways of doing this are (a) including the target word more than once; (b) taking away any numbering system; (c) putting the distracters on the same

level as the initial target word; and (d) using different fonts (see Appendix below).

2. This procedure uses only bona fide words of English. Some writers suggest a variation on this exercise which is more like a proofreading task: The distracters are the target word with some typing error introduced (omission of letter, addition of letter, inversion of letter order).

3. This procedure is most useful if you use it in conjunction with a textbook you use in other classes. This way you can build up a battery of exercises you will be able to use with future classes as well.

Appendix: Word Recognition (Timed Exercise)

WORD RECOGNITION (Timed exercise)

In each exercise, circle the word – or words – which are the same as the ones printed in bold.

1 **instantaneous**
instantaneous instantiation spontaneously instantaneous instantaneously

2 **humiliating**
humiliation fumigation humidifying humiliated humiliating

3 **affectionate**
affective affectation affection affectionate affectionate

4 **aggression**
aggressive aggressively aggression attention aggregation

5 **physical**
physical physiological physically fiscal physically physics physical

6 **psychologist**
psychiatrist psychology psychiatry psychoanalyst psychologist

7 **breeds**
breed bread breed breeds creeds breeds

8 **cowardly**
cowardice cowardly cowards outwardly cowardice

9 **response**
respond responsive response respite reasonable

10 **disease**
diseases diseased deceased disease desist

From Paran, A. (1991). *Reading comprehension, year 1.* Burlington Proficiency Series. Burlington Books. Page 35 used with permission.

Contributor

Amos Paran, a doctoral candidate at the University of Reading, England, is an Israeli teacher interested in doing research on and writing about reading.

Strategies for Coping With Vocabulary

Levels
Intermediate +

Aims
Develop strategies for coping with unfamiliar vocabulary

Class Time
No set time

Preparation Time
No set time

Resources
Appropriate reading materials
Overhead projector and transparencies

Proficient readers routinely make decisions on how to process the new or unfamiliar vocabulary they encounter as they read. Less proficient readers lack such strategies and waste time searching through dictionaries for definitions of words they do *not* need to know to understand a given piece of reading. This activity encourages them to practice effective strategies.

Procedure

1. Select reading materials that are roughly appropriate for the reading ability level of the students.
2. If possible, prepare an overhead transparency of several paragraphs of the material. If this is not possible, provide copies for each student.
3. Discuss with the students the strategies you want them to learn.

   - For example, some new words may be safely ignored or skipped because their meaning contributes little to the main idea of the reading material: If the purpose of a reading is to give an overview of a country's exports, one may read something like, *Country X exports a variety of ores and minerals such as tin, copper, iron, bauxite, etc.* We assume the new word is *bauxite.* The efficient reader skips the word bauxite knowing from the context that it is either a metal or a mineral, and for the purposes of understanding the reading, that is sufficient. To interrupt the reading and look up the meaning in a dictionary is an inefficient reading practice.
   - The second strategy is to recognize new words which are defined by the context in which they appear. For example: *Malaysia is an exporter of bauxite ore from which aluminum is extracted.*

The context in this case clearly defines what bauxite is. Thus there is no need to look up the meaning of the word.

- The last strategy is to identify words which are not defined by context and the understanding of which is necessary for comprehension of the passage. For example: *Bauxite is Malaysia's single most important export.* In this case, bauxite is not defined by context, it is clearly something of importance to Malaysia's economy, and therefore understanding it is important. When this kind of vocabulary is encountered, the student will need to have recourse to a dictionary or seek assistance from a resource person. But before doing this, the student should read ahead a few lines to see if the context eventually defines the meaning of the word.

4. Working with a transparency of the material and an overhead projector, identify those words which are unknown to a majority of the students. For a few examples, show the students which words may safely be ignored, which are defined by context, and which must be researched for their meaning. Shift to a testing mode and ask the students to identify the words that fall into the three categories. Work either with the class as a whole or divide the class into groups and have the groups make the decisions.

5. If desired, pass out short passages (or use a transparency) that contain all three categories and test the ability of the students to recognize them. This should be a culminating activity, used only after the students demonstrate that they are doing well at recognizing the different categories of words.

Contributor

Ted Plaister taught in the Department of ESL, University of Hawaii for 24 years. He has also taught in Thailand, Japan, Micronesia, and American Samoa.

Developing Word and Phrase Recognition Exercises

Levels
Beginning and intermediate

Aims
Provide students with opportunities to improve their reading recognition skills

Class Time
5–7 minutes

Preparation Time
No set time

Resources
Class readings

Recent reading research has indicated that accurate, rapid, and automatic recognition skills often distinguish skilled readers from less skilled readers. Furthermore, much research indicates that "comprehension deficits can at least in part be traced to deficiencies within the word recognition process" (Chabot, Zehr, Prinzo, & Petros, 1984, p. 148). This activity exercises students' word and phrase recognition skills.

Procedure

Development of Word/Phrase Recognition Exercises

1. In order to develop an exercise with 20 items, select 20 key words from a reading passage that students will read, are likely to read, or would be interested in reading.
2. For each key word, generate a string of five words that will serve as a recognition exercise item; one of the five words in the string should be identical to the key word. The other words will serve as distracters. For example:

Key word

thorough	through	thorough	thought	though	tough
smiled	smelled	sweet	smoked	sweated	smiled

3. When ordering the string of words for each key word, be sure to place the identical word in different positions (at the beginning, in the middle, or at the end of the string).
4. When selecting distracters, keep the following variations in mind:
   - Morphological variations of the same word

prove	proved	proves	proven	prove	proves
give	gave	gives	give	given	giving

- Similar letter clusters

look	hook	cook	took	book	look
hike	like	mike	hike	bike	dike
strike	streak	strike	steak	stroke	spike

- Reordered letters

| *meat* | team | tame | meat | mate |

- Similar orthographic form

thorough	thorough	through	thought	though	tough
moon	noon	moon	soon	cocoon	room
disturb	distress	dislike	disturb	distant	distill
hands	bands	lands	hands	sands	fans
wheat	whale	where	wheel	wheat	what

- Random variation

| *babies* | bounds | drowned | babble | bubble | babies |
| *sister* | system | disaster | stern | sister | sisters |

It is not uncommon for all these variations to be incorporated into a recognition exercise comprising 20 key words.

5. At the bottom of the exercise page, provide students with a means for keeping track of their time and accuracy. For example:

Time: _____ seconds

Number correct: _____ /20

6. Phrase recognition exercises can be written by following these same guidelines. Because of space limitations on the page, it is advisable to include four phrases rather than five after the key phrase. For example:

Key phrase

in the hall	at the hall	in the fall	on the ball	in the hall
at the bend	at the beam	at the bend	at the bank	in the band
in a jar	in a jam	for a job	in a jar	on the jar
for the prince	for a price	in the rice	for his price	for the prince

Classroom Procedures

1. Do word/phrase recognition exercises regularly throughout a semester or school year. After the first introductory period—during which

you (a) explain the overall importance of developing efficient reading skills, (b) give a rationale for these exercises, and (c) explain and practice the procedure—devote only a few minutes to the recognition exercises. Students will learn to

- start when you say to begin (ideally when the second hand of the classroom clock is on the 12)
- look at the key word/phrase in the left-hand column
- move eyes to the right as quickly as possible to identify the identical word/phrase
- cross out the identical word/phrase and then quickly move on to the next line, for example:

  flowers   flavors   flow/ers   floats   floods   favorite

- look up at the clock and record exact time (in seconds and/or minutes) needed to finish at the bottom of the page;
- correct answers and mark down the number of mistakes on the bottom of the page.

Three recognition exercises should be done consecutively. The first can be considered a warm-up exercise; students then strive to proceed faster and more accurately with the last two. Start out with word recognition exercises and later have students do phrase recognition exercises. With both types of exercises, students have fun, improve their recognition skills and their reading in general. (See Stoller, 1986, for other procedural suggestions.)

Caveats and Options

Recognition exercises should not be confused with vocabulary expansion exercises; nor should they be seen as a substitutes for reading passages. They are simply exercises that help students develop speed and perceptual accuracy with a limited amount of classroom instruction time.

References and Further Reading

Chabot, R. J., Zehr, H. D., Prinzo, O. V., & Petros, T. V. (1984). The speed of word recognition subprocesses and reading achievement in college students. *Reading Research Quarterly, 19*, 147–161.

Stoller, F. L. (1986). Reading lab: Developing low-level reading skills. In F. Dubin, D. E. Eskey, & W. Grabe (Eds.), *Teaching second language reading for academic purposes* (pp. 51–76). Reading, MA: Addison-Wesley.

Contributor

Fredricka L. Stoller is Assistant Professor in the English Department and Director of the Program in Intensive English at Northern Arizona University, in Flagstaff.

♦ Dictionaries
Learning to Use the Dictionary

Levels
High beginning and low
intermediate

Aims
Increase vocabulary
through use of a
bilingual dictionary

Class Time
45 minutes, two
separate classes

Resources
Lesson entitled
"Learning to Use the
Dictionary"

Students need vocabulary in order to express themselves. They are motivated to acquire it and can help themselves find what they want to say when they can use their own bilingual dictionaries to look up unfamiliar words. This is a lesson to savor because the rewards are enormous. It can be a real breakthrough toward greater literacy.

Procedure

1. Work closely with the students. Students of low literacy may never have used a dictionary. In Part 1 of the lesson (see Appendix below), Alphabetizing, read along with them, pointing out the words and letters of the words they are looking up, so they may grasp the idea of alphabetizing.
2. In Part 2, Using the Dictionary, have students open their dictionaries to the letter *B*, where they can see that the letter *A* is the second letter. At the bottom of this first paragraph they will look up words beginning: *bab, bac, bad, bag*. In the second paragraph they will turn to words beginning with letters *be* and will look up words beginning with *bea, bed, bef, beg*. In the third paragraph they turn to words beginning with *bi, bic, big, bil, bir*. At this point, they will be utilizing what they learned in the previous step.
3. If they have not caught on to the procedure, continue until they do. In Part 3, Dictionary Work, instruct them to use the guide words at the top left and right of each page. This last step is based upon the two previous steps and is the thrust of the lesson.

**Appendix:
Sample
Dictionary
Lesson**

Learning to Use
the Dictionary

I ALPHABETIZING

Use the alphabet to help you do the following exercises.

a b c d e f g h i j k l m n o p q r s t u v w x y z

1. Put these letters in correct order:

    b c a   ___ ___ ___

    i g h   ___ ___ ___

    o m n   ___ ___ ___

2. Put these words in correct order according to their first letters:

| sit | baby | light | house | ___ ___ ___ ___ |
| fast | apple | cake | down | ___ ___ ___ ___ |

3. These words have the same first letter. Arrange them according to their second letters:

buy	big	boy		___ ___ ___
pin	pan	put	pet	___ ___ ___ ___
shell	sell	spell		___ ___ ___

4. These words begin with the same two letters. Put them in order according to their third letters:

plan	plum	plot	___ ___ ___
flock	flake	flute	___ ___ ___
street	stamp	stop	___ ___ ___
through	thought	thin	___ ___ ___

II USING THE DICTIONARY

Open the dictionary to where the letter 'b' begins. Notice that the first words you see following the 'b' all have 'a' for their second letter. Now look at their third letter. Notice that these third letters follow in alphabetical order: first 'a', then 'b', then 'c', through the rest of the alphabet. Using this idea, let's practice and look up the following words: baby, back, bad, bag.

Now turn the pages and pass the letters 'ba' until you find words beginning with 'be.' Look up these words: beach, bed, before, begin.

Now continue turning pages until you find words starting with 'bi.' Find these words: bicycle, big, bill, bird.

Now look for these words: black, boat, brake, bud.

III DICTIONARY WORK

Open the dictionary and look at the top of any page. You can see two words in dark letters. The word on the left gives you the first word on the page. The word on the right gives you the last word on the page, and between these, all words are in alphabetical order, according to their second, third, fourth, etc. letters.

Let's practice finding some words. Turn to the letter 'b' and look for the word 'bad.' You know it is close to the beginning of the 'b' because its second letter is 'a.' It comes after words beginning with 'bab' and 'bac' because 'b' and 'c' come before 'd' in the alphabet.

Let's try another word. Turn to the letter 'n' and find the word 'not.' The second letter, 'o', of 'not' is more towards the middle of the alphabet, so you must pass words beginning with 'na', 'ne', 'ni', and find words beginning with 'no.' Now you need to find the third letter, 't', after the 'o.' Look for it in its alphabetical order at the top of the pages in dark letters.

Using what you know, you can now look up any new words in the dictionary as you read.

From Bailey, J. (1988, 1992). *Begin in English*. Vols. 1 & 2. Studio City, CA: JAG Publications. Pages 12-13 used with permission.

Contributor

Joan Ashkenas is the publisher and editor of JAG Publications, which specializes in ESL and bilingual teaching materials.

Getting to Know Your Dictionary

Levels
Any

Aims
Introduce or practice using dictionaries as a source of information
Learn how to identify the suitability of the dictionary for one's needs

Class Time
5 minutes–1 hour

Preparation Time
30–45 minutes

Resources
One quality dictionary for the teacher and different dictionaries for each student

Students often ask which dictionary they should buy or whether a particular dictionary is a good one. Through this activity, they find out how to locate information in various dictionaries and the advantages and disadvantages of their personal dictionaries. It is important to point out the inadequacies of bilingual dictionaries. A particular problem is understanding concepts students have not learned in their first language.

Procedure

Decide which information is important for students in their future work and prepare a handout with appropriate exercises. For example:

1. Inconsistencies in British and American English
   What is the American word or expression for *chemist*, *flat*?
2. Pronunciation and Parts of Speech
   What is a *sow*? What is a *doe*? Do these words rhyme?
3. Irregular Plurals
   What is the plural of *crisis*? Of *radius*?
4. Irregular Verbs
   What is the present tense of *spat*? Of *partook*?
5. Transitive and Intransitive Verbs
   Place an *X* next to each group of words that is a complete sentence (i.e., nothing must be added to complete the meaning):

   _____ They lynched
   _____ The storm abated
6. Usage
   Fill in the missing word (preposition or particle) in the sentence *if* it is necessary.

We should all abide _____ the rules.

He ascertained _____ the fact.

7. Expressions

Use the expression in a sentence which shows its meaning.

the bane of (my) existence

in harms way

8. Acronyms and Abbreviations

What is: *WHO* or *lbs.*?

9. Register

Circle the words that you would *not* use in a university essay:

quark, googol, snot, discombobulate

10. Foreign Phrases

What is the meaning of the following?

nom de plume, post facto, in vitro

11. Current Expressions

What is a *byte*, a *yuppie*?

Caveats and Options

1. We divided the students into groups so that different kinds of dictionaries were represented in each group (e.g., an electronic dictionary, a bilingual dictionary, a pocket dictionary).

2. You can have groups race each other and can offer a prize to the first group that finishes the exercise with all of the correct answers.

Contributors

Joyce Friedler and Beverly A. Lewin are coordinators of the English for Humanities program in the Division of Foreign Languages, Tel Aviv University, Israel.

◆ Cohesion
Cohesive References

Levels
Any

Aims
Raise awareness of the various types of cohesion in texts

Class Time
15–20 minutes

Preparation Time
30 minutes

Resources
A class text

Many types of cohesion exist in an English text. A reader must successfully identify the different cohesive links in the text to comprehend the text fully. This activity presents an alternative way of looking at cohesive devices in texts. It goes beyond a simple comprehension exercise by raising the students' awareness of the types of grammatical and lexical cohesion in English texts.

Procedure

1. Locate different types of reference in the text: lexical referents, possessive pronouns, personal pronouns, demonstratives. Extract those sentences and type them out. Underline the cohesive devices or type them out in bold.
2. Make a list of the types of cohesive devices used in the examples. This can be done using fairly simple metalanguage (see Appendix below).
3. In class, ask students to identify, for each sentence typed, which cohesive device is being used, and what exactly is being referred to.

Contributor

Amos Paran, a doctoral candidate at the University of Reading, England, is an Israeli teacher and materials writer interested in doing research on and writing about reading.

Appendix: Sample Cohesion Activity

ORGANISING TEXTS AND IDEAS

The extracts below use three different ways of connecting sentences and references:

a Grammatical reference

b A synonym or near synonym referring to precise noun phrases mentioned previously

c A new noun phrase summarising a whole topic mentioned previously

For each of the words or phrases in bold, decide which technique is being used, and what is being referred to. Refer to the text where necessary.

1   ...**the moment of transition** will actually occur on December 31, 2000 ... (lines 11-12)   _____

2   ...**the anniversary** will find mankind toying with intimations of mortality. (lines 16-18)   _____

3   ...the Scythian monk, Dionysius Exiguus, who devised **it** ... (lines 24-25)   _____

4   In fact, **these tales** seem largely to have been the invention ... (lines 44-45)   _____

5   Even if **they** had, they would have been unlikely to gather ... (lines 52-53)   _____

6   ...**a term** that has itself now become synonymous with modernity. (lines 75-77)   _____

7   **The decisive reply** came five years later ... (lines 93-94)   _____

8   ...**others** from the past were retrieved from neglect. (lines 102-103)   _____

9   ... could fulfil **its** potential. (line 109)   _____

10   Speaking of **the work's** final scene, its first conductor, André Messager ... (lines 115-116)   _____

From Paran, A. (1991). *Reading comprehension, year 2*. Burlington Proficiency Series. Burlington Books. Page 79 used with permission.

Track the Noun

Levels
Intermediate +

Aims
Raise awareness of
anaphoric relations

Class Time
10–15 minutes

Preparation Time
20–30 minutes

Resources
A reading text the class
is analyzing

Cohesive devices are an important feature of texts because they help readers construct a meaningful representation of texts in their minds. Readers must be able to follow the referents of different pronouns (i.e., personal, demonstrative, or relative) as well as those of the referents of noun phrases in order to construct such representations. Because different languages achieve cohesion in different ways, this is an important skill for students to practice. This is also a pleasurable way of doing what can become a boring comprehension question.

Procedure

1. Choose an important noun or noun phrase in a passage that is repeated many times or that is referred to frequently.
2. For yourself, write out each occurrence of the noun (or noun phrase) as well as each pronominal reference. Note the line number for each occurrence or reference.
3. Draw a matrix similar to the one in the example (see Appendix below). Adjust the number of boxes on the matrix to the number of times the noun occurs or is referred to.
4. Write out the first occurrence of the noun and the line in the first box. In the following boxes, either write out the word, or leave the box empty. Leave the majority of boxes empty.
5. After you have read the text in class and possibly done a number of exercises on it, ask the class to fill in the matrix by finding each reference to the noun, using the hints provided.

Caveats and Options

1. In some cases, it may be best to supply line numbers in some of the boxes. In other cases (e.g., where there are many repetitions of the same pronouns), it is possible to give line numbers only.

2. This type of matrix can also be used to highlight lexical cohesion (e.g., the occurrence in the text of a large number of nouns belonging to the same semantic field) or to bring out temporal relations in the text.

3. Teachers may want to check this in class. However, in contrast to most pronoun reference exercises, this one does not really need checking. If students have made mistakes, they usually find out that they have not filled in all the boxes or that the word printed in the box does not tally with the word on their list—which means that they have made a mistake earlier on. Thus, the exercise is self-correcting. The most it needs is for students to compare their answers quickly with those of a classmate.

4. It is also possible sometimes to extract some of the rules of pronoun reference from the examples, and the exercise can thus connect to the students' own writing.

Appendix: Sample Cohesion Activity

Since the articles you are reading are about cats, the writers will clearly refer to cats many times. Sometimes they will use nouns, sometimes they will use pronouns and sometimes they will use possessives. Make a list of all the references to "cat" or "cats" in FIRST READING. Use the diagram below, part of which is already filled in for you.

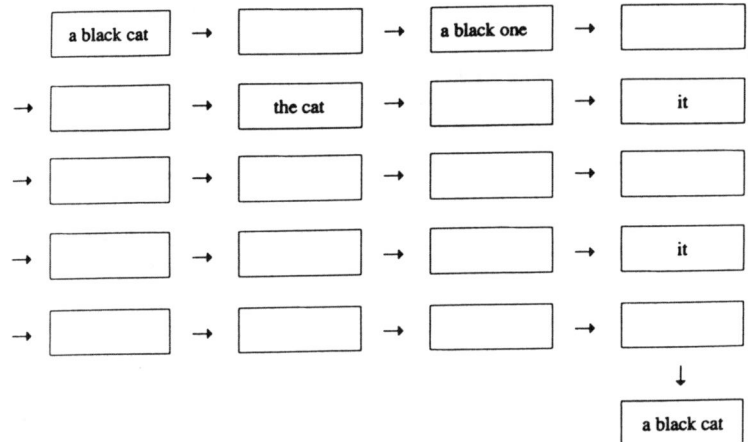

From Paran, A. (1991). *Reading comprehension, year 1.* Burlington Proficiency Series. Burlington Books. Page 11 used with permission.

Contributor

Amos Paran, a doctoral candidate at the University of Reading, England, is an Israeli teacher and materials writer interested in doing research on and writing about reading.

◆ Games for Young Readers
The Food Label Store

Levels
Beginning; ESL
primarily, but can be
adapted for EFL

Aims
Involve students in the
development of their
own reading skills
Help students see a
connection between
reading in school and
reading in the outside
world

Class Time
No set time

Preparation Time
20–30 minutes

Resources
One or more cardboard
boxes, depending on
how large the store is
to be
Glue or staples
A series of questions
about food labels

Students may be more motivated to learn if they become involved in their own learning and if they can generalize what they are learning in class to activities outside the classroom. Shopping for food is a relevant activity for nearly any student.

Procedure

1. Tell the students to bring to class food labels of any description (e.g., labels from cans, meats, bottles, jars; fronts of boxes of cereals, mixes, soap, milk containers; wrappers from loaves of bread, rolls).
2. Place the students in whatever size group you think works best (anywhere from three to six students works well) and give each group a cardboard store.
3. Have them glue their labels to their store.
4. When the groups have finished creating their stores, ask a series of questions that the students can answer by reading the labels from their stores. Sample questions include: *What food is the most expensive? The cheapest? Which product is the heaviest? The lightest? Which food do you like best? Why? The least? Why? What two foods go together (e.g., salt and pepper, bread and butter, peanut butter and jelly)? How many brands are there of the same product?*
5. You might also have the students do a variety of tasks. For example, ask them to find as many brand names as they can as quickly as

possible. Another task is to have them add up the total cost of all of the products in the store. Or ask them to put all of the products in various categories (e.g., meats, dairy products).

Caveats and Options

1. Have the students work with stores that other groups created.
2. Distribute the questions and have the students write their answers.
3. Ask the questions orally and have the students write their answers.
4. Have them make up a menu for a particular meal.
5. This activity can deal with products other than food. For example, you could have students bring in ads for clothes or small appliances. It can be adapted to an EFL situation if students have access outside the classroom to products with English labels. Or you could collect labels and bring them to class for the students to use in making the stores.
6. If there is limited space and storing the boxes is difficult, use poster boards instead of cardboard boxes.

Contributor

Richard R. Day, whose early EFL experiences include the Peace Corps in Ethiopia, is Professor of ESL, University of Hawaii.

Bingo™ and Othello™ for Beginning Readers

Levels
Young learners who already know the alphabet and some basic phonics

Aims
Make finding, recognizing, and reading the written form of already familiar items rewarding through games of chance or skill

Class Time
5–10 minutes

Preparation Time
No set time

Resources
Bingo™ grids of 9, 16, or 25 squares with words or phrases in the squares
Place markers, such as poker chips or coins of low denomination

Using games that are available commercially saves teachers valuable preparation time. In addition, students may be familiar with them, which is a great benefit in explaining the rules of the games. This activity uses two popular games that are popular with young children.

Procedure

The first student to get a complete, straight line of squares marked off on a Bingo™ card wins. You can either call out the word (e.g., *Eight*), give hints (e.g., *The number of legs that spiders and octopuses have*), ask questions (e.g., *How many legs does an octopus have?*), or provide unfinished sentences (e.g., *Spiders have _____ legs.*).

Caveats and Options

1. Distribute word cards (9, 16, or 25 to each student) and have students arrange them into their own grid configuration. Simpler yet, students could have, for instance, one row of five cards each, with the first student to get all five called being the winner. Place markers aren't necessary with word cards as students can simply turn a card over when it is called.

2. This game is like the commercially sold game Othello™. It is only like Bingo™ in that cards are laid out in a grid and colored markers (preferably poker chips) are used. Word cards are laid out (ideally, 36 or more) and students all play this one grid. Students play against each other to capture the most squares. They can place a marker of their particular color on any open square if they can read it. They capture squares when they place a marker (e.g., blue) on a square and in so doing sandwich any other colored markers in a straight line between the one just laid and another one previously laid. Two students can play (e.g., blue vs. red) but the game is more exciting when three or more colors are involved. If there are more students than colors, teams of two or three can be made.

3. It will save time if a copy machine is used to make Bingo™ sheets; just rearrange small word cards on the glass to print out a different configuration. Students can make and fill out Bingo™ grids themselves, but at that level, the game might be too easy for them.

4. The original Othello™ game is published by Tsukada Corporation.

Contributor

Matthew Taylor has taught in Nagoya, Japan for many years and has recently obtained an MA TESOL degree from Columbia University Teachers College, Tokyo.

Discard Game Variations

Levels
Young learners who
already know the
alphabet and some
basic phonics

Aims
Make finding and
recognizing the written
form of already familiar
items fun and rewarding

Class Time
5–15 minutes

Preparation Time
No set time

Resources
Deck of prepared cards

Fluent reading depends on automatic decoding. This activity helps young readers build their decoding skills in a game that increases their motivation and interest.

Procedure

1. Create a deck of cards comprising any of these paired sets:
   - pictures (e.g., noun, action)/word, phrase or sentence that describe a picture word, phrase or sentence in learners' first language/the same word, phrase or sentence in learners' target language
   - Arabic number/written number
   - numbers from 1–12/names of the corresponding months
   - question/answer
   - a word that can be paired with an opposite/its opposite

   The cards used should be small enough to hold like playing cards. If the material is being prepared from scratch, use blank cards, making them from larger sheets of construction paper if they are not commercially available.

2. Seat a group of 3–10 students around a large table or several desks moved together. Ask students to play individual hands, or pair up and share a hand with a partner.

3. Divide the stack of cards into matching halves. Take one of the halves, shuffle it, and deal it out to the students. One at a time, show or call out cards from the other half. Whichever student has the card matching the one showed or called discards it. The first student to discard all cards wins.

Caveats and Options

1. All cards (both halves) are shuffled and dealt out. First, students are asked to discard any matching pairs already in their hand. Play starts

when the student, say, to your left discards one (any card). Whichever student has the card matching that one discards it, then discards the next one (any card). And so on, until one winning student is the first to discard his/her last card.

2. With either the first game or Option 1, objects (beanbags work well) are put in the center of the table, one object less than the number of students playing. When any student plays his/her last card, all students rush to grab the objects in the center. One student, the "dumbbell," will not be able to grab an object.

3. Option 1 can become somewhat like the card game Uno™ if you prepare and put into the deck some extra cards such as "Reverse" (which changes the direction of play), and "Skip 1," "Skip 2," "Skip 3" (i.e., pass over that number of players in the current direction of play), and so forth. Another rule borrowed from Uno™ could be that a player must say, "Uno!" (or any word) when playing his/her penultimate card. The penalty for not saying it is drawing two (or three or four) cards. If Option 1 is so modified, the sequence of play must also be altered. That is, in Option 1, the next player is determined more or less randomly. In this version, play must proceed clockwise or counter-clockwise, although this doesn't apply to students who are laying down the second half of a matching pair. For instance, a student plays a 7. Anybody who has the word *seven* plays it. In Option 1, the next student to play would be the person who played *seven*. In this version, the next student to play would be the student to the left or right (depending on the current direction of play) of the student who played 7.

4. Option 3 is not as complicated as it may sound, and making the Uno-like cards is very easy. These cards add a lot of suspense and strategy to the game. They can also be stored separately and used with any other deck of matching pairs that you have.

Contributor

Matthew Taylor has taught in Nagoya, Japan for many years and has recently obtained an MA TESOL degree from Columbia University Teachers College, Tokyo.

Grab Game Variations

Levels
Young learners who already know the alphabet and some basic phonics

Aims
Make finding and recognizing the written form of already familiar items rewarding through fun and competition

Class Time
5–10 minutes

Preparation Time
No set time

Resources
Word cards (i.e., cards with a single word, a phrase or a sentence on them)

This activity helps young readers increase their automatic decoding skills. Because it is played in the form of a game, student interest and motivation are high.

Procedure

1. Seat 3–10 students around a table, or several desks moved together, or a section of floor.
2. Spread the word cards out on the floor. Tell students that as you read one of the word cards aloud, they should rush to grab it. The student with the most cards at the end wins.

Caveats and Options

1. This activity would recycle any of the matching pair cards mentioned in Discard Game Variations (previous entry, this volume). Spread out the cards of either half of a matching group. Instead of calling out one of the cards, simply show a card from the other matching half. Students rush to find and grab the card that matches the one shown. For instance, in the case of pictures and words, all of the word cards are laid out. As you show the picture cards one by one, students try to grab the matching words. This is, of course, reversible; the picture cards could be spread out, and the word cards could be shown one by one.
2. This variation would again use any of the matching pair cards mentioned in the first Option 1. Students are in teams. The cards of either half of a matching group are face down on one side of the room. The other half is face up on the other side. Students run to the face-down cards, grab one, then run to the other side of the room to find and

grab the matching card. The team with the most matching pairs at the end wins. This can be organized either like a relay (teams lined up, and only one student from each team making a run at any given time), or a free-for-all (all students dashing back and forth across the room at the same time). In the latter case, it is not necessary to use teams; all students could be competing against everyone else.

3. This is a somewhat more involved version of the previous option, but definitely worth trying. Students are in two teams. Each team has caller(s) and grabber(s). Half of a matching group of cards is spread out face up on one side of the room. The other half is in one stack, face down, on the other side of the room. Callers of both teams draw from this one stack and call out the drawn card to their team members on the other side of the room. These grabbers grab the card that matches the one called and run to the callers to hand it over to them. When the callers have a matching pair in their hand, they can draw another card, which they in turn call out to their grabbers on the other side of the room. After about 5 minutes of yelling and dashing back and forth across the room, one team will end up with the most correctly matched pairs.

4. For the simple grab game and Option 1, sharp students can easily dominate, so it is good to periodically remove them from the competition somehow (for example, by making them callers instead of the teacher).

5. It is possible in Options 1–3 to use triple matches instead of pairs. Ray and Masumi Ormandy, for instance, have published a *Daily Expressions* set (Pacific English Club, Tokyo) which features an expression in English on one card, in Japanese on another, and an illustration of the expression on another. Option 3, in particular, works well with the game focused on three different parts of the room and three different kinds of cards.

Contributor

Matthew Taylor has taught in Nagoya, Japan for many years and has recently obtained an MA TESOL degree from Columbia University Teachers College, Tokyo.

◆ Miscellaneous
Color the Sound

Levels
False beginning

Aims
Distinguish vowel
sounds
Reinforce the
association of vowel
sounds with particular
letters or combinations
of letters

Class Time
30 minutes

Preparation
No set time

Resources
Cassette player
Cassette tape with
familiar song
Handout with lyrics of
the song
Crayons or light
colored markers

Students are often confounded by the seeming lack of connection between the spoken and written word. It is important that the student recognize that there is a connection, albeit a complex one. This activity takes advantage of many students' love of singing to make its point.

Procedure

1. Prepare a handout of the lyrics of the song. Underline letters that represent vowel sounds (e.g., *in my Easter bonnet, with all the frills upon it...*).
2. Play the tape.
3. Give each student a copy of the handout sheet and a set of colored markers or crayons. (The number of colors depends on how many sounds you want to deal with. I recommend keeping the number low initially. As you go along you can always add more.)
4. Play the tape a second time, this time with the students following the words on their handout sheets.
5. Have the students take a particular crayon or marker, say, a red one. Tell them to color the letters that represent a particular sound, say, the /i/ sound as in *with* or *frills*. Play the tape a third time. If the class is good, you might want to try two or three sounds with two or three colors.

6. Divide the class into groups of two or three and have them discuss and compare their sheets. Ask for a volunteer from a particular group to present the result to the class.
7. Repeat Steps 4 and 5 with different colors and different vowel sounds.
8. Once some or all of the vowel sounds are colored (it's not necessary to do this at one sitting) have the class sing the song—with or without the tape—following the words on their sheets.

Caveats and Options

1. Pick a particular word, *Easter*, for example, and ask the students to write as many words as they can in 3 minutes, in which the sound /iː/ is represented by the same *ea* letter combination—*each* or *leave*, for example—or by a letter, or combination of letters other than *ea*: for example, *e* as in *me*, *y* as in *many*, or *ei* as in *receive*.
2. This type of lesson can be expanded to practice distinguishing between voiced and unvoiced consonant sounds, for example, the difference between the *th* in *with* and the *th* in *the*.
3. Whether the students understand the meaning of the song is of secondary importance. If they don't, you may want to work this out with them at some point. However, the emphasis should be on connecting sounds and their symbols, not on meanings.

Contributor

John Pettet, a teacher and writer specializing in media applications in ESL/EFL, taught English in Italy for 20 years. He is, at present, freelance writing in New Jersey.

Reading a Letter From a Pen Pal

Levels
Beginning +

Aims
Practice reading for
questions
Practice prereading

Class Time
45 minutes

Preparation Time
1 hour's work spread
over 2 weeks

Resources
Letters from a class of
students at another
school

This activity can provide students with their first personal use of written English. When the students realize that the letters were written especially for them, their motivation for reading can increase.

Procedure

1. In preparation, contact an ESL teacher in a different city who has students of a similar level. Make an agreement that you will exchange letters, and that students will read and reply to the letters they receive. Ask the other teacher to send the student letters in a bulk package to you. (The letters should contain self-introductions, questions for the reader, and sentences telling what the writer is most interested in.)
2. Pass out the letters that you have received from the other school. If there are too few letters, choose a few students to work as pairs and share the work of reading one letter. (If there are extra letters, they can be given to students who want to do additional homework after class.)
3. Have the students read aloud the name of the pen pal. Ask the class to guess the gender and nationality of the writer.
4. Ask the students to read the first paragraph of the letter. Suggest that they circle key words. Ask if they have learned the right answer to the writer's gender and nationality.
5. Have the students underline the questions asked in the letter. Let groups of three or four students compare the questions in their letters. Which are different and which are the same? Have the groups compile lists of the questions asked in the letters they received.

6. Suggest that each student look for sentences that tell what the writer of their letter is interested in. Repeat Step 5 with the writers' interests substituted for questions.
7. Follow up this activity with a writing activity: replying to the letter from their pen pal.

Caveats and Options

1. Have the students read letters from other members of their class.
2. This activity can be followed by real-life or contrived business letters requesting information.

Contributor

Hugh Rutledge graduated from Boston University. He has taught in East Asia for 4 years and is Head of Faculty at Tokyo International College, Japan.

Reading Roulette

Levels
Any

Aims
Practice reading for pleasure using vocabulary learned from previous classes
Practice reading and writing in a timed setting

Class Time
1 hour

Preparation Time
5 minutes

Resources
List of good topic sentences

It is important to recognize topic sentences in paragraphs for reading and writing activities, as they are a key to understanding the text. This activity combines the search for topic sentences with speed reading and peer correction. Students also have a break from reading materials in textbooks. They read their own material and feel a sense of pride. They laugh a lot as they read what their classmates have written. They have fun.

Procedure

1. Create groups of three to five students. All groups should have equal numbers.
2. Give all students the same topic sentence (complete or incomplete): *It was a dark and stormy night and . . . .*
3. Have students write for 3 minutes.
4. After 3 minutes, have them pass their papers to the classmate on their right (within their group).
5. Give students 4 minutes to read what was written by their classmate and then continue to write from where their classmate left off.
6. Give them 5 minutes to repeat Step 5.
7. Increase the time after each exchange of papers and keep repeating Step 5.
8. Return the papers to the original writer, who will write the conclusion.

   The original writer now has an essay to read which was written by that student and classmates.
9. If there are five students in a group, the total time spent on reading and writing should be $3 + 4 + 5 + 6 + 7 + 8 = 33$ minutes. The first 3 minutes and the last 8 minutes will be utilized by the original

writer, who will write the introduction and conclusion. The four other group members will write four paragraphs.

10. Each student now has a student-generated piece of reading (a total of six paragraphs).

Caveats and Options

Students can peer correct essays with teacher monitoring.

Contributor

Davi J. Spencer teaches at the Language and Culture Center, University of Houston, Texas. She has also taught English in Japan.

Part III: Oral Reading

Oral Reading—A Fresh Look

Contributor's Note

Throughout much of the world, learning English means learning to read English. In many classes, a major part of this effort is spent having students read aloud. Unfortunately, as it is usually done, the benefit to learners is questionable. Often oral reading means one student reads while the others (supposedly) listen. The reader is under pressure and is so nervous that it is unlikely much is being learned. The others, if they're listening at all, are waiting for the reader to make a mistake. The other model, choral reading, is of equally dubious merit. Typically done with the belief that it somehow improves learners' pronunciation, the reality is a few students read clearly while a large number simply mumble along in a sing-song drone.

Despite these problems, oral reading remains popular, even standard in most foreign language situations, in part because nonnative-English-speaking teachers whose English ability may not be at the level they would like perceive it as something that they and their students can actually accomplish. In some places, oral reading is even seen as progressive, replacing strict grammar-translation where little English was ever spoken at all.

In addition to those reasons, there are some aspects of reading in which oral techniques can actually build specific skills. Native-English-speaking children are generally encouraged to read aloud in school. It is likely that, at the beginning levels, this helps with sound/spelling correspondence. Another area where oral reading can be useful is in learning to chunk or read in phrases and units of meaning:

Wedon'treadlikethis.

Rather, // we read // in meaningful chunks.

We all do this naturally in our native languages. It's a skill we developed in part by being read to and hearing the phrasing of our parents, teachers and older siblings. And it's a skill that EFL readers can practice in class.

In spite of these benefits, oral reading remains one of the most roundly criticized foreign language teaching techniques. Warnings in the literature range from the imperative "Don't!" to the gentler, if somewhat ominous, "Be careful." And indeed, some caution is needed. Oral reading is necessarily slower than silent reading and the lack of speed is one of the biggest problems foreign/second language readers face. For this reason, reading aloud should only be a minor part of the students' reading curriculum. A second major problem is that it is virtually impossible to read aloud and focus on meaning at the same time. Reflecting that, the activities presented in this section are primarily post-reading exercises that give the students further opportunity to work and interact with a text in a meaningful way. Perhaps the most serious problem with traditional oral reading is that it lacks real pedagogic purpose. Those who are reading have nothing approaching a task (except, perhaps, the desire to finish one's section without looking foolish). Those who listen, if they do so at all, don't need to understand or react to what they hear.

Oral reading does and will take place in the EFL classroom. The activities that follow are an attempt to move away from the traditional models while building on the advantages that reading aloud can provide. They aim to make reading aloud more effective—and more interesting—by engaging learners in tasks that allow them to interact with the meaning of the text and with each other.

Marc Helgesen
Miyagi Gakuin
Sendai, Japan

Catching the Chunks

Levels
Any

Aims
Identify phrases/
meaning units

Class Time
5–10 minutes

Preparation Time
10 minutes

Resources
Two worksheets, *A* and
B, each containing five
paragraphs from a text
the learners have
already read

Efficient readers process information in sense-groups (meaning-based segments) rather than word-by-word. Activities that increase their awareness of phrasing as a cue to chunking meaning are useful.

Procedure

1. Before class, prepare the first paragraph of your own copy of the text by reading it aloud to yourself. Put a slash at each pause. For example, the first two sentences in this paragraph would appear as follows: *Before class / prepare the first paragraph / of your own copy / of the text / by reading it aloud / to yourself. / Put a slash / at each pause.*

    Do not mark the pauses for Paragraph 1 on the student worksheet. Prepare worksheet A by marking the pauses with slashes on Paragraphs 2 and 4. Mark Paragraphs 3 and 5 on worksheet B. Make an even number of copies. Half the learners need the A sheet. Half need the B sheet.

2. In class, have the students look at the first paragraph. Read it to them, having them draw a slash each time you pause. Then they read the paragraph back, telling you where to put the slashes.

3. Divide the class into pairs, *A* and *B*. Each learner needs the appropriate worksheet.

4. In their pairs, the learners who have Worksheet *A* read Paragraph 2 while those with Worksheet *B* listen and mark the phrasing. Then *Bs* check by reading back the paragraph, indicating where the slashes were put.

5. *Bs* then read Paragraph 3 while *As* listen and mark. The procedure continues until they have finished.

Caveats and Options

1. As learners have become proficient at the technique, have them decide on their own where they would pause. This helps make them more aware of the way form and structure contribute to meaning since pauses usually come between the subject and the verb, around propositional phrases.
2. The first few times you try this, you may be unsure where to put the pauses. This is because texts read aloud to different audiences for different purposes are phrased differently. Trust your instincts.
3. Although this technique doesn't lead to particularly smooth speaking/reading, the result is more natural than the sing-song word-by-word reading students usually do in oral reading.
4. Limit the use of the activity to a short time, done on a regular basis.

Find the Mistakes

Levels
Any

Aims
Make meaningful
changes in a text and
recognize those changes
when listening to a
reading of the text

Class Time
5–10 minutes

Preparation Time
1–2 minutes

Resources
A text learners have
previously read, one
copy per learner

Frequently, students don't listen to each other during oral reading activities. This activity creates the need for them to listen to each other. Also, since the oral reading is done in pairs, it is more time efficient and less threatening than when one student reads to the entire class.

Procedure

1. Before class, glance over the first paragraph of the text you'll be using. Decide on two or three of the words in the text that you could substitute with other words having different meanings. Write the words to be substituted next to the changed words. For example, the first sentence of this paragraph could become: *Before class, glance over the first page of the text you'll be using.*
2. In class, have the learners look at the text. Tell them you are going to read the text but will make some "mistakes." They should listen and try to catch your mistakes.
3. Read Paragraph 1, substituting the words as planned in Step 1. Students listen for the mistakes. They can either underline the words that were different from what you said or, at a somewhat higher level, try to catch exactly what you did say.
4. Once they understand the procedure, divide them into pairs, *A* and *B*. Tell *A* to silently read Paragraph 2 and decide on two or three changes. *B* does the same with Paragraph 3.
5. Partners then read their respective paragraphs to each other, catching their partners "mistakes."

Caveats and Options

1. Don't change words by using synonyms or words with nearly the same meaning (e.g., *have to/must*). You want learners thinking about meaning here, not just words.

2. One problem that often occurs with oral reading is that the reader is overly worried about making mistakes. By framing the activity as "find the mistakes" rather than "find the differences," learners are given a cover when they really do misread something. Partners don't know if the mistake was really an error or an intended change.

Whistle Dictation Creativity Contest

Levels
Any

Aims
Test comprehension
Have learners add their
own ideas to a text

Class Time
10–15 minutes

Preparation Time
3–5 minutes

Resources
A paragraph of text
previously read

Dictation, though out of fashion in many circles, is still used throughout most of the world. Too often, however, learners find it boring. This activity has them interact with the dictation text.

Procedure

1. On your copy of the text, underline or delete all examples of one part of speech, for example, descriptive adjectives. Other words may be deleted to increase interest. Example:

   A _____ road ran through a _____ forest. A _____ man was walking down the road. Suddenly he saw a _____ woman. She was wearing a _____ coat and a _____ hat. She looked at him and said _____ .

2. In class, dictate the paragraph to the learners. When you get the blanks/underlined words, whistle or say "blank" instead of the words (e.g., A (whistle) road ran through a (whistle) forest.).

3. Have learners write the paragraph, adding whatever word they think appropriate.

4. Divide learners into groups of four or five. They take turns reading each sentence. Any time a student has filled a blank with a word than no one else has used, that answer is deemed "creative" and the student gets a point. If all the learners in the group have different words for a given blank, they each get a point. The learner with the most points is the winner. In their groups, learners can veto words that don't fit or call on the teacher for a judgment when they aren't sure.

Caveats and Options

1. Distribute copies of the paragraph with the blanks in place. Learners read silently and fill in the blanks as they would with any cloze-procedure activity. Then they do the "creativity contest" (Step 4) to compare.

2. The activity tests comprehension because learners need to understand the paragraph in order to write appropriate words. It can be used to test previously read material by deleting, for example, all the verbs. Learners should fill in the words that fit. There is no reason that the learners should guess the exact word deleted from the text. Words not from the original but that make sense should be allowed.

3. This is a variation on a technique learned from Mario Rinvoluccri.

Split Dictation

Levels
Any

Aims
Identify sentence-level
organization

Class Time
10 minutes

Preparation Time
5 minutes

Resources
A paragraph from a text
the students will
subsequently read

During most dictations, learners need focus only on the words rather than on the overall meaning of the text. The activity requires them to think about meaning as they listen, write, and read what they have already written.

Procedure

1. Before class, select a paragraph to be dictated. For example:

   When he was a boy, Tom Cruise could not read. He couldn't understand the words. Sometimes they seemed backward to him. Because he couldn't read, he didn't do well in school. Now, Tom Cruise loves to learn.

   You will dictate the paragraph in sections. Divide it as follows:

   First dictation: When he was // Tom Cruise // could not // the words. // backward to him // Because he // he didn't do well // in school // to learn

   Second dictation: a boy // read. // He couldn't understand // Sometimes they seemed // couldn't read // Now, // Tom Cruise loves

   You can easily divide the paragraph by using two different colored highlighting marking pens, one for each dictation. While dividing the text, be sure not to alternate simply between the first and second dictations. In some instances, adjacent parts of sentences should be in the same dictation, divided by pauses (e.g., in the first dictation: Tom Cruise // could not).

2. In class, read the first dictation as the learners write. They should leave spaces wherever you pause (//). Then give the second dictation. Learners write it, inserting the phrases in the correct position in what they have already written.

Caveats and Options

1. Once learners know the procedure, you can prepare copies of the separate dictations and have them work in pairs, dictating to each other. If the dictation phrases are divided according to chunks (phrases each containing one "sense-group"), it reinforces the phrasing strategy suggested in Catching the Chunks (this volume).
2. I learned this technique from Alan Maley.

References and Further Reading

The sample text is from Helgesen, M., Brown, S., & Venning, R. (1991). *Firsthand success*. Longman/Lingual House. Used with permission.

Getting the Rhythm

Levels
Any (especially for learners whose mother-tongue is not stress timed)

Aims
Identify stress patterns

Class Time
15–20 minutes

Preparation Time
5–10 minutes

Resources
A poem or song with a reasonably even rhythm that the learners have previously read, one copy per learner
Optional: either an overhead projector transparency with the text on it or additional copies of the text with the stress identified

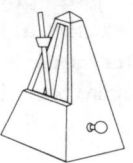

Learners often have difficulty with the stress timing of English, particularly if their mother tongue is syllable timed. The activity can help familiarize them with the rhythm of English and can make reductions easier. The activity is effective because the rhythm of most song and poems follows the natural stress of English. By keeping the rhythm, learners force themselves to reduce the other words appropriately. Marvin Gaye's classic "I Heard It Through the Grapevine" (Motown) is an example of a song that works particularly well.

Procedure

1. Before class, read the text aloud (or, in the case of a song, listen to it). Mark the stress on your copy by underlining the stressed words.
2. In class, read the text (or play the song) to the students. They mark the stress on their copies. It may be necessary to do this twice.
3. Compare their answers with yours by (a) having the class read the text aloud together, marking the stress by tapping on their desks; (b) displaying the transparency and having them tell you which words to mark; or (c) distributing copies of your version, stress indicated.
4. Divide the class into pairs, A and B. As act as "human metronomes," snapping their fingers or tapping their desks in an even rhythm. Bs read the text aloud, attempting to keep the rhythm by saying the stressed words on the beat and fitting the other words in between the stresses. They then change roles.

Note: Stress timing means that stressed syllables usually occur in an even rhythm. The other words, however many there are, fit between those even stresses. This results in reduced forms. English is fairly, though not completely, stress timed. Some other languages, Japanese and French for example, are syllable timed. Each syllable tends to be the same length.

271

As Fast as You Can

Levels
Beginning +; primarily EFL

Aims
Oral warm-up

Class Time
5–10 minutes

Preparation Time
None

Resources
One or two paragraphs of a previously read text, one copy per learner

This articulation activity gives learners practice reading aloud quickly. It is most useful as a quick warm-up before another reading or oral activity.

Procedure

1. Read the text aloud quite rapidly as the learners read along silently. Check your time to see how long it takes to read.
2. Write the target time on the chalkboard:

   Target time = Your reading time x 5 + 30 seconds
   This target time will be the students' speed goal.

3. Have learners draw five small circles on a piece of paper.
4. When you tell them to start, ask all learners to read the paragraph aloud (to themselves) as rapidly as they can. Each time they finish the paragraph, they draw a line through one of the circles.
5. At the end of the target time, tell them to stop. Learners check to see how many of the circles they crossed out.

Caveats and Options

1. To do the activity as a game, don't set a target time. Just have learners race to be the first to read the paragraph five times.
2. It is also possible to do the activity in pairs or groups of three, each reading in turn as in a relay. If this option is used, the target time should be changed to allow for six, rather than five, readings.
3. This is strictly an articulation/warm-up activity, much like a physical warm-up before sports. As such, it is impossible for learners to focus on meaning or answer comprehension questions afterwards.
4. The teacher who taught me this activity credited Fukiko Shincho of Shogen JHS, Sendai, Japan, with its origin.

Stress/Stand Up

Levels
Beginning

Aims
Help students identify
stressed syllables in
words

Class Time
5–10 minutes

Preparation Time
None

Resources
A chalkboard
Any text all the learners
are reading

Word stress can be an important aspect of vocabulary. In this activity, students focus on stress. It also gives students an opportunity to self-select vocabulary they want to work with.

Procedure

1. After the learners have read a text, elicit from them vocabulary they found new, difficult, or interesting. List the items on the board, separating single-syllable words from the others. You will be using the longer words.
2. Say each word. Pause for about one second, the cue the students to repeat the word, standing as they say the stressed syllable. For example, if the word is *photographer*, students stand when they say /ta/ and quickly sit down when they get to /gr /.

Caveats and Options

1. If a reading is accompanied by a specific list of words the students are to learn, prepare two worksheets. Each sheet has all of the words, half of which have the stress marked. Learners work in pairs. The one with the words marked reads them while the partner repeats and stands.
2. This activity is particularly useful for students whose mother-tongue makes little use of stress within words. It can also help students overcome the problem of English words borrowed into their native languages with different pronunciations.
3. "Stress/Stand Up" makes use of Total Physical Response by having the students engage in "full body" learning. Doing the action makes it easier to remember the words.

One More Time, With Feeling

Levels
Any

Aims
Encourage expression
in oral reading

Class Time
5–10 minutes

Preparation Time
None

Resources
A chalkboard
A copy of one or two
paragraphs of any text,
one copy per student

Learners reading aloud often do so with little feeling and affect. This activity can help them develop expression. The feelings they choose may or may not be related to the text. It is quite possible, for example, to read an exciting passage while you're tired.

Procedure

1. With the class, brainstorm a list of emotions and physical states (e.g., excited, happy, bored, tired, hung over). Write them on the board.
2. Have learners select the paragraph or paragraphs they will read. They also choose one of the feelings listed on the board. Tell them they will read the selection as if they felt that way.
3. They practice reading the text aloud (to themselves).
4. In pairs or small groups, they read the selection. Partners try to guess the feeling.

Dialogues: Variations on a Theme

Levels
Any

Aims
Vary the practice of
reading dialogues orally

Class Time
No set time

Preparation Time
No set time

Resources
Sample dialogues

The use of prepared dialogues is perhaps the most common and certainly the most widely accepted use of oral reading. Dialogues have several strengths. They provide a context which makes comprehension easier. They serve as a model of real interaction. They can move learners into a role play or fantasy experience that relaxes some learners and removes the seriousness and inhibition that may come with studying English. They are often short enough for students to master, not in the sense of memorization but as something that can be read several times until learners become comfortable with them.

Dialogues are not, of course, without their problems. Although dialogues can be interesting and motivating, often they are not. At times, in an effort to make grammar or functions clear, they are unnatural. A major problem is that dialogues are essentially frozen speech. They never change although real communication requires a great deal of flexibility. Also, in many textbooks they are so common that, when practice is done in a standard way, they become boring. Clearly, bored students pay less attention; inattentive students don't learn much.

The way readers practice is important. In many parts of the world, it is common to have one group read a dialogue in front of the entire class. Although this may be useful at the end of dialogue practice, it is generally an inefficient way to work with the conversation because most learners won't get enough time to really work with the text. Also, the merits of having a few students perform in front of the others need to be considered. It's said that the average person is more afraid of public speaking than of going to the dentist. With that kind of anxiety level, it is questionable how much the performers are really learning.

What follows are ways to vary the practice of reading dialogues orally. In most cases, it is assumed all students will be practicing in pairs or small groups at the same time. The use of any particular option will, of course, depend on the specific dialogue. Nonetheless, all are ways to breath life—and communication—into what might otherwise be strictly mechanical practice.

Procedure

For the examples that follow, let's assume the students are reading this simple dialogue that takes place in a clothing store:

Shopper: Excuse me. I'm looking for a sweater.
Clerk: What size?
Shopper: Large, I think.
Clerk: Here's a nice one.
Shopper: How much is it?
Clerk: It's fifty-five dollars.

The following suggestions change the text of the dialogue above. Text here is meant to include both variations in the written form learners see and change, sometimes student generated, in what is actually said.

1. Excuse me? Elicit from the learners repetition or clarification phrases such as *Excuse me?, Could you repeat that?, Pardon?* and *I'm sorry?* and write them on the chalkboard. As learners read the dialogue aloud, they imagine they are in a very noisy place. It is hard to hear their partners so they have to ask for repetition regularly. When they do, their partners repeat the previous line. As a variation, the person asking for repetition repeats or paraphrases the line after hearing it a second time (e.g., *Shopper: Excuse me. I'm looking for a sweater. Clerk: Pardon? Shopper: I'm looking for a sweater. Clerk: A sweater? What size?*).

2. Recreate the dialogue. Read the dialogue (or play a tape) to the learners two or three times. The students then work in groups of two or three and attempt to write the conversation they heard. It isn't important for students to write it exactly; this isn't a dictation. Rather they should try to write a conversation with basically the same meaning. They then look at the text, note their changes, and try to determine, among themselves or by asking you, if their variations are acceptable ways to say the same thing. They then practice their version of the dialogue (as corrected if necessary). For extra

support, you may want to list the basic functions within the dialogue on the chalkboard (e.g., greet, invite, ask about time, etc.).

3. Split conversations. Many students practice dialogues as if they were two parallel monologues. Rather than listening to each other, they read their lines and then prepare for their next part. To encourage listening, redo the text by making one copy for each person in the conversation. On each copy, use correction fluid to eliminate all the sentences except those for a given speaker. Make copies so each learner can have one. As students practice, they must listen to each other to know when to read their next line. In conversations with more than two speakers, this technique also checks comprehension as students must understand the dialogue to know when to say a given line.

4. Find the conversation. Write or modify dialogues so that, after the first line, each speaker has two possible responses, only one of which makes sense. For example, a shopping dialogue might begin as follows:

> Shopper: Excuse me. I'm looking for a sweater.
> Clerk: a. What are you looking for?
>   b. What size?
> Shopper: a. Large, I think.
>   b. Blue I think. (etc.)

Speakers must read both choices silently and listen to their partners to find the conversation—know which response to read aloud. This variation can easily be combined with the split conversation strategy above.

5. Slots. To increase student flexibility and to ensure listening, add substitutions for various words in the dialogue. To do so, underline particular words, number them, and write the two or three substitutions for each in the margin or on the chalkboard. For example, in the shopping conversation, *sweater* could be underlined. Substitutions could include *shirt* and *jacket. Size* could be replaced with *color* and *style.* As learners practice, they read the substitutions rather than the words that originally appeared. Students must listen to each other in order to respond to the substitution choices used.

Caveats and Options

1. Several of the ideas in this section call for making copies in order to vary the text style. If you are working with dialogues from a textbook, copying is, of course, illegal. However, when considering copyright violations, publishers normally consider intent. Books should never be copied to avoid having the students buy them. If, on the other hand, you choose to create a variation on the presentation in a book your students have each purchased, it's unlikely you'll have any problems with the publisher. If you have any doubt, contact the publisher's representative.

2. Have learners stand and face each other while practicing. Standing makes gesturing and eye contact easier. Also, when learners are making eye contact, they have to look away from the text. This helps build memory.

3. To encourage eye contact and to cut down on over reliance on the text, do two-person dialogues in groups of three. Only one person has the book. That student—the reader—acts as the "human tape recorder" by whispering the lines to the respective speaker who, in turn, say them to their partners. The "tape recorder" can repeat the lines as often as necessary. After once or twice through the dialogue, partners change parts and begin again.

4. Have learners wait to speak until they have strong eye contact with their partners. They can look back at the text as often as necessary but they can't speak unless they wait for eye contact. As mentioned in Option 2, this helps with memory. It also encourages students to listen to their partners rather than simply preparing for their own next line.

5. A variation on the above technique is to have one learner try very hard to maintain eye contact. The other tries to avoid it.

6. For telephone conversations, have learners stand back to back. As with a real phone conversation, they can't see each other.

7. To encourage learners to speak more loudly, have them face their partners, then take one step back so there is at least 1 meter of space between them. Getting students to speak more loudly helps

break the pattern of soft, emotionless "classroom talk" some students use. It also seems to build confidence.

8. In a dialogue about an object such as a photograph or a newspaper schedule, have the readers use a single copy of the book. They pass it back and forth as if it were the real object. That encourages them to interact. As they do so, they become less tied to the text. It is also possible, of course, to use a real object and act out the conversation.

9. It's not uncommon to be doing a parallel action unrelated to the topic of conversation as we speak. Write a list of actions such as tying one's shoe, cleaning a desk, and drinking coffee. As they practice the conversation, learners do or pantomime the actions. A variation is to list items like hiccups, and nervous tics (e.g., biting one's lip, drumming fingers, tapping one's foot). Learners do the actions as they practice.

10. Learners, in parallel lines, face each other and practice the dialogue. Then the people in one line move one person to the right and the person at the end moves to the other end of the line. They do the dialogue again with the new partner. This continues until they have had a given number of partners. If you want to encourage speed, have the same number of people in each line. For example, if you have 40 students, you could have either 4 lines with 10 students each or 8 lines of 5. Learners race to be the first line in which people in one row practice the conversation with each student in the parallel row.

11. Students often use the same, fairly flat register when they speak English in class. The following are some contrasting voice and characterization options that can help learners experiment with their voices. The options can also increase student interest and enjoyment. As they read a two-person dialogue, each learner does one of the following:

- acts shy or nervous versus outgoing and confident
- acts bored or sleepy versus excited or energetic
- acts happy versus sad

- acts "too" helpful or concerned. The other is put off by the level of interest. (This is useful in dialogues about giving advice.)
- uses high versus low pitch
- uses fast versus slow speed

The dialogue variations presented here are all ways to get the students more interested and involved while they read and practice dialogues. They help the students move beyond simply reading aloud. They can create a situation where students really interact and communicate with each other.

Also available from TESOL

All Things to All People
Donald N. Flemming, Lucie C. Germer, and Christiane Kelley

*A New Decade of Language Testing Research: Selected Papers from the
1990 Language Testing Research Colloquium*
Dan Douglas and Carol Chapelle, Editors

A World of Books: An Annotated Reading List for ESL/EFL Students
Dorothy S. Brown

Children and ESL: Integrating Perspectives
Pat Rigg and D. Scott Enright, Editors

Coherence in Writing: Research and Pedagogical Perspectives
Ulla Connor and Ann M. Johns, Editors

*Dialogue Journal Writing with Nonnative English Speakers:
A Handbook for Teachers*
Joy Kreeft Peyton and Leslee Reed

*Dialogue Journal Writing with Nonnative English Speakers:
An Instructional Packet for Teachers and Workshop Leaders*
Joy Kreeft Peyton and Jana Staton

*Directory of Professional Preparation Programs in TESOL in the
United States, 1992–1994*

Diversity as Resource: Redefining Cultural Literacy
Denise E. Murray, Editor

Ending Remediation: Linking ESL and Content in Higher Education
Sarah Benesch, Editor

Research in Reading in English as a Second Language
Joanne Devine, Patricia L. Carrell, and David E. Eskey, Editors

Selected Articles from the TESOL Newsletter: 1966–1983
John F. Haskell, Editor

Students and Teachers Writing Together: Perspectives on Journal Writing
Joy Kreeft Peyton, Editor

Video in Second Language Teaching: Using, Selecting, and Producing Video for the Classroom
Susan Stempleski and Paul Arcario, Editors

For more information, contact

Teachers of English to Speakers of Other Languages, Inc.
1600 Cameron Street, Suite 300
Alexandria, Virginia 22314 USA
Tel 703-836-0774 • Fax 703-836-7864